The Winning Delegate

The WINNING DELEGATE

An Insider's Guide to Model United Nations

KEREM TURUNÇ

iUniverse, Inc.
New York   Bloomington

The Winning Delegate
An Insider's Guide to Model United Nations

iUniverse books may be ordered through booksellers or by contacting:

iUniverse
1663 Liberty Drive
Bloomington, IN 47403
www.iuniverse.com
1-800-Authors (1-800-288-4677)

Because of the dynamic nature of the Internet, any Web
addresses or links contained in this book may have changed
since publication and may no longer be valid.

ISBN: 978-1-4401-4430-1 (pbk)

Printed in the United States of America

iUniverse rev. date: 12/3/2009

Contents

PREFACE

My background in Model United Nations began in high school, at the American Collegiate Institute in İzmir, Turkey, where I helped found my school's first Model UN club. I had spent the previous summer at a university's summer-school program, in which I met people involved in Model UN. What I had heard interested me very much, and when I returned to my high school, I found out there had been plans for some time to form a Model UN team and that there were two faculty members who were interested in starting it. Together, we formed a small team, which made its debut at the Turkish National Model United Nations and then went to the famous THIMUN (The Hague International Model United Nations), a huge conference that lasts an entire week and draws over three thousand students from over two hundred schools around the world.

I enjoyed my high school experience greatly, so when I went to college, I sought out the Model UN organization, run by the Yale International Relations Association (YIRA). Soon, I realized I was spending a good deal of my time outside of classes with my involvement in YIRA. Eventually, I devoted over thirty hours each week in preparations when I was Secretary-General of the Yale Model United Nations. Keep in mind, however, that you can spend much less time participating in Model UN and still have a great experience.

During my time at Yale, I also served as the Vice-President of YIRA, chaired committees at the Security Council Simulation at Yale, Yale's collegiate Model UN conference, and won best delegate awards at various national conferences as a member of the Model United Nations Team at Yale.

To this day, I still use the skills I developed or improved thanks to Model UN, skills such as public speaking, negotiation, and research. I now want to share some of my experience and expertise with others so that readers would find their Model UN experience as fulfilling as mine was. I enjoyed reflecting on my experiences and writing this book immensely, and I hope you enjoy reading it.

Kerem Turunç

ACKNOWLEDGMENTS

While developing this book, I asked for and received help from many people, whose recommendations greatly strengthened the final version.

Many thanks to Stuart Berkman, a dear family friend, who took time to read and comment on the manuscript and will find many of his ideas incorporated here.

A big thanks to Sinae Han, my Yale classmate and fellow MUNer, for her valuable opinions and input.

Finally, I thank my parents, Onur and Noyan Turunç, without whose love, faith, and encouragement, I never could have completed this book.

CHAPTER ONE:

INTRODUCTION

I.   About the United Nations

When U.S. president Franklin Roosevelt and British prime minister Winston Churchill founded the Atlantic Charter in 1941, they probably could not foresee that sixty-eight years later, as many as 192 sovereign nations would sit in the General Assembly of an international organization called the United Nations (UN). The original Atlantic Charter called for the "fullest collaboration between all nations in the economic field."[1] Although this seemed uncomplicated at first glance, the implications of the charter were really not so simple.

How did this Charter evolve over the years into a colossal international organization, encompassing almost all nations of the world as well tens of agencies and related organizations as diverse in their field of work from each other as UNICEF, IMF, and UPU?[2] An even bigger question, of course, is why was the United Nations founded at all?

International organizations date back to the early nineteenth century. The first such organizations were the river commissions in Europe. These were followed by the International Telegraphic Union in 1865 and the Universal Postal Union in 1874. Then came the Hague Conferences of 1899 and 1907, which endeavored to establish an international law system on which a new world order

---

1   Robert E. Riggs and Jack C. Plano, *The United Nations: International Organization and World Politics* (Fort Worth: Harcourt Brace College Publishers, 1994), 12.

2   United Nations Children's Fund, International Monetary Fund, and Universal Postal Union, respectively.

could operate. But none of these attempts was aimed at forming a political entity that would have continuous operation. Only after World War I did such an organization come into being: the League of Nations (1919–1939). The founder of the League was U.S. president Woodrow Wilson, whose stated goal was to achieve a world order based on peace and democracy. The League had forty-two founding members. Until its dissolution, another twenty-one nations became members at different times but the maximum number of members at any time was fifty-eight.

Ironically, the United States never became a member of the League. Wilson did not play his domestic political cards adroitly and failed to convince the U.S. Congress to join the international organization, even though it had been founded by the American president. The lack of participation of the United States is still regarded as the single most important reason why the League did not live long. The League was helpless when Japan attacked Manchuria (part of China) and when Italy invaded Ethiopia, and it drew its last breath when Hitler attacked Poland in September 1939. An organization founded to prevent another war had its hands tied behind its back as a new war unfolded.

On January 1, 1942, Washington, D.C. witnessed the signing of the United Nations Declaration by twenty-six nations. The term "United Nations" was first used by Roosevelt to refer to these twenty-six who, by signing the declaration, approved and demonstrated their support for the Atlantic Charter and pledged to fight against the Axis Powers (Germany, Italy, and Japan). The Declaration was later signed by twenty-one other nations, forming a much stronger alliance in opposition to the Axis powers during World War II.

Then followed the Moscow Declaration of October 30, 1943, in which the "Big Four" nations (China, the Soviet Union, the United Kingdom, and the United States) agreed on the principle of forming an international entity to preserve global peace. In November of the same year, Franklin Roosevelt, Winston Churchill, and Joseph Stalin met in Tehran to confirm once again their commitment to this goal.

The Bretton Woods Conference of July 1-22, 1944 led to the creation of the International Monetary Fund and the World

Bank (then called the International Bank for Reconstruction and Development). These two Bretton Woods institutions later became integral parts of the United Nations System.

Shortly thereafter, the Dumbarton Oaks Conference was held by the Big Four in a mansion at Dumbarton Oaks, Washington, D.C. between August 21 and October 7, 1944. All four powers already agreed on the need to form an international organization after the end of the war. What they were unsure of, however, was how to structure this new organization. After much debate, the draft Charter of the United Nations, which the United States had already been working on before the Conference, became what is known as the Dumbarton Oaks Proposals.

Then followed the Yalta Conference, which lasted from February 4 to 11, 1945. At Yalta, Roosevelt, Churchill, and Stalin met to discuss unresolved matters from Dumbarton Oaks. With much debate on issues such as trusteeship and membership of the various republics of the Soviet Union, the parties agreed to hold another conference in San Francisco on April 25, 1945.

Later that year, fifty nations attended the United Nations Conference on International Organization (San Francisco Conference) in San Francisco to finalize the Charter. The agenda was fundamentally consideration of the Dumbarton Oaks Proposals and some five hundred amendments to it. On June 26, 1945, the Charter of the United Nations was signed by the fifty participants (Poland, which is an original member, signed it later that year). After ratification by China, France, the Soviet Union, the United Kingdom, the United States, and a majority of the other signatories, the Charter went into effect on October 24, 1945 (now universally celebrated as United Nations Day).

The structure of the Charter was very similar to the Covenant of the League of Nations. Both the Covenant and the Charter were written with the ostensible aim of global peace and order based on some sort of international law. Both organizations had three main bodies: an assembly, a council, and a secretariat. Additionally, the International Court of Justice of the League was adopted by the United Nations, and the Mandates Commission founded under the League became the Trusteeship Council. However, the major difference between the League and the newly founded United Nations was that membership in the UN was universal. All nations, small or large, were able to join this new organization so long as they complied with the basic notion of peace. Accordingly, self-determination was an integral part of the Charter, a notion lacking in the Covenant of the League.

Today, the United Nations still operates under the same Charter with minor amendments. The organization has been indispensable in facilitating international cooperation and action since its founding. However, the UN is not a world government, and membership in it is completely voluntary. Nevertheless, it is the closest existing thing to a world government, and states recognize its legitimacy in resolving disputes through peaceful means.

Article One of the first chapter of the Charter designates the purposes of the UN as:

1. to maintain international peace and security
2. to develop friendly relations among nations based on respect for the principle of equal rights and self-determination of peoples
3. to achieve international cooperation in solving international problems and in promoting and encouraging respect for human rights and for fundamental freedoms for all
4. to be a center for harmonizing the actions of nations in the attainment of these common ends.

Article Two of the first chapter sets the principles to be followed to realize these purposes:

1. the sovereign equality of all its members
2. that all members will fulfill their obligations in accordance with the Charter
3. that all members will settle their international disputes by peaceful means
4. that all members will refrain in their international relations from the threat or use of force against any other state
5. that all members will give the UN every assistance in any action it takes in accordance with the Charter, and will refrain from giving assistance to any state against which the UN is taking preventive or enforcement action
6. that the UN will ensure that nonmember states act in accordance

with these principles so far as may be necessary for the maintenance of international peace and security

7. that nothing contained in the Charter will authorize the UN to intervene in the domestic matters of any state.

The UN System

The term the *United Nations System* refers to the extensive and complex network of entities that is made up of the main bodies (called the principal organs) of the UN, the commissions and programs reporting directly to these organs, and the specialized agencies (autonomous intergovernmental organizations linked to the UN by special agreements).

All but one of the six principal organs are located at the UN Headquarters in New York. The sixth principal organ, the International Court of Justice (ICJ), operates in The Hague, the Netherlands. The other entities of the UN System have their own governing bodies, budgets, and secretariats, and their branches and operations are spread through the world.

You will note that some of the terms and names used in this book are spelled using British English while I have otherwise employed American English spelling throughout the book. Such deviations are intentional in order to respect the official spelling that the UN or the particular entity uses.

Principal Organs

The **General Assembly (GA)** is *the* main organ of the United Nations. All UN members are represented by up to five delegates in the GA. Each member has one vote that is equal to the vote of each of the other members. Such a structure makes the GA the closest thing to a world parliament, even though this would be a misnomer, as the GA does not legislate but simply recommends courses of action. At best, these recommendations have moral binding power on member nations. So, it would be more accurate to call the GA a world forum that is used by nations to express their views on various issues. In addition to member nations, several observer groups sit in on GA proceedings and voice their opinions on the issues at hand, although they are not permitted to vote.

The GA holds its regular session from September to December of each year, and when it is out of session, work still goes on through its six main committees and their respective subsidiary organs, as well as within the Secretariat. When necessary, the GA can hold emergency or special sessions or resume its current suspended session.

The six committees of the GA are:

- First Committee: Disarmament and International Security
- Second Committee: Economic and Financial
- Third Committee: Social, Humanitarian and Cultural
- Fourth Committee: Special Political and Decolonization
- Fifth Committee: Administrative and Budgetary
- Sixth Committee: Legal

In addition to the main committees, the General Assembly's subsidiary bodies also include:

1. several boards (such as the Trade and Development Board)
2. commissions (the Disarmament Commission, the International Civil Service Commission, the International Legal Commission, the United Nations Commission on International Trade Law, the United Nations Conciliation Commission for Palestine, the United Nations Peacebuilding Commission, and the Advisory Commission on the United Nations Relief and Works Agency for Palestine Refugees in the Near East)
3. various standing, ad hoc, advisory, executive, high-level, and special committees (such as the Committee against Torture, the Committee on the Elimination of Discrimination against Women, the Committee on the Peaceful Uses of Outer Space, the Ad Hoc Committee on the Elaboration of a Convention Against Corruption, the Advisory Committee on Administrative and Budgetary Questions, the Executive Committee of the Programme of the United Nations High Commissioner for Refugees, the High-level Committee on the Review of Technical Cooperation among Developing Countries, and the Special

Committee on the Charter of the United Nations and on the Strengthening of the Role of the Organization)
4. councils and panels (such as the Human Rights Council)
5. various standing, open-ended, and open-ended ad hoc working groups (such as the High-level Open-ended Working Group on the Financial Situation of the United Nations, the Open-ended Working Group on the Question of Equitable Representation on and Increase in the Membership of the Security Council and Other Matters Related to the Security Council)
6. certain other subsidiary bodies (such as the United Nations Open-ended Informal Consultative Process on Oceans and the Law of the Sea)

Perhaps the most controversial, yet one of the most important, subsidiary bodies of the General Assembly is the United Nations Human Rights Council (HRC), established in 2006 by an almost-unanimous General Assembly vote to replace the Commission on Human Rights.[3] The Human Rights Council has forty-seven rotating members—thirteen from the African regional group, thirteen from the Asian regional group, six from the Eastern European regional group, eight from the Latin American and Caribbean regional group, and seven from the Western European and Others regional group.

The Human Rights Council's mandate is to promote "universal respect for the protection of all human rights and fundamental freedoms for all, without distinction for any kind and in a fair and equal manner."[4] It has been criticized (like its predecessor), mostly by Western countries, for focusing excessively on the Israeli-Palestinian conflict and for its inclusion of member countries with poor human rights records.

Every year, the General Assembly discusses and makes recommendations on well over a hundred international issues in a wide range of fields. These include cooperation in economic, cultural, social, educational and health fields, human rights, development of international law, disarmament, maintenance of peace, and the

---

3   The only votes against the establishment of the Human Rights Council were cast by Israel, the Marshall Islands, Palau, and the United States. Belarus, Iran, and Venezuela abstained.

4   UN General Assembly, Sixtieth Session, Resolution 251, A/RES/60/251, March 15, 2006.

environment, as well as internal matters such as overseeing the work of other UN bodies, annual budget approvals, and appropriations. The GA also elects the Secretary-General based on the recommendation of the Security Council. Also on the recommendation of the Security Council, the GA admits new members and is also authorized to expel members.

Voting in the GA is by simple majority except on "important questions," which require a two-thirds majority vote. Chapter IV, Article 18, Clause 2 of the UN Charter defines important questions as recommendations with respect to the maintenance of international peace and security, the election of the nonpermanent members of the Security Council, the election of the members of the Economic and Social Council, the election of members of the Trusteeship Council, the admission of new members to the United Nations, the suspension of the rights and privileges of membership, the expulsion of members, questions relating to the operation of the trusteeship system, and budgetary questions.

Since GA resolutions are not binding and come in the form of recommendations and opinions, more support for a decision makes it more legitimate as the opinion of the world community and more difficult for countries not to comply with it because of the moral pressure it exerts. As such, it is best if decisions are reached by consensus, which has been happening more frequently since the end of the Cold War.

The **Security Council's (SC)** main responsibility is maintaining international peace and security. As such, it is the only organ in the UN System with binding executive power. To fulfill its duty, the Security Council can meet anytime it deems necessary. When dealing with a conflict, it first tries peaceful means such as negotiation, mediation, establishing a ceasefire, and peacekeeping. If such methods do not work, the Security Council can impose partial or total sanctions, and, as a last resort, authorize collective military action as it did during the Korean War and against Iraq after its invasion of Kuwait in 1990.

The Security Council has no readily available matériel, forces, or arms, and therefore, member states are expected to contribute necessary equipment and personnel to execute its decisions. The Security Council can also take preventative action by investigating potential threats to international security and stopping them before they arise.

The Security Council consists of fifteen members. Originally there were eleven, but the number increased in 1965 through an amendment to the Charter. Five are permanent members: China, France, the Russian Federation, the United Kingdom, and the United States. The other ten are elected by the GA for two-year terms, with five new members chosen each year.

Approval of any motion by the Security Council requires nine affirmative votes, and in all nonprocedural matters, a "no" by any permanent member constitutes a veto. The only exception to this rule is that members are required to abstain from voting on resolutions calling for peaceful means of settlement (Chapter VI of the Charter) in a conflict to which they are a party.

With changing world balance and expanded membership in the UN, many nations are discontent with the membership and voting structures of the Security Council. There have been various studies and proposals by the UN and other institutions to restructure the Security Council, but so far there is no consensus on the nature of a restructuring. Recommendations include, but are not limited to, abolishing the veto, limiting its use, establishing new permanent seats (with or without veto power), expanding the size of the Security Council, giving more power to developing and least-developed countries, and creating regional permanent seats to be occupied in a rotating manner by regional powers.

The **Economic and Social Council (ECOSOC)** coordinates the economic, social, humanitarian, and related work of UN's specialized agencies and makes recommendations to member states on these issues. Its membership is limited to fifty-four states (increased from the original size of 18 members) that elected by the GA for three-year terms. Eighteen members change each year.

ECOSOC meets in several sessions throughout the year and has a major session each July, which alternates between New York and Geneva, during which ministers and other high officials meet to discuss major economic, social, and humanitarian issues.

ECOSOC encompasses five regional economic commissions that work to promote economic development and economic cooperation in their respective regions, nine functional commissions, as well as three standing committees.

The regional commissions are the Economic Commission for Africa (ECA), headquartered in Addis Ababa; the Economic and Social Commission for Asia and the Pacific (ESCAP), headquartered in Bangkok; the Economic Commission for Europe (ECE), headquartered in Geneva; the Economic Commission for Latin America and the Caribbean (ECLAC), headquartered in Santiago; and the Economic and Social Commission for Western Asia (ESCWA), headquartered in Beirut.

The functional commissions are the Commission for Social Development, the Commission on Crime Prevention and Criminal Justice, the Commission on Narcotic Drugs, the Commission on Population and Development, the Commission on Science and Technology for Development, the Commission on Sustainable Development, the Commission on the Status of Women, the Statistical Commission, and the United Nations Forum on Forests.

The three standing committees are the Committee for Programme and Coordination, the Committee on Non-Governmental Organizations, and the Committee on Negotiations with Intergovernmental Agencies.

In addition to these subsidiary bodies, the ECOSOC system also includes several ad hoc and expert bodies on various topics. Another function of ECOSOC is to consult with academics, business sector representatives and over 1,600 Non-Governmental Organizations (NGOs) that perform ECOSOC-related work around the world. Some of these NGOs take part as observers in the meetings of ECOSOC and its subsidiaries.

The **Trusteeship Council (TC)** was created to oversee and prepare eleven UN Trustee Territories—regions without their own governments administered by member states under the Trusteeship System—for independence and self-government. The Trusteeship Council is no longer active as all of these territories are now either independent states or have joined neighboring independent countries. The last trust territory, Palau, was admitted as the 185th UN member state in 1994 after which the TC suspended regular meetings and operations. Membership in the Trusteeship Council is now composed of the permanent Security Council members who meet occasionally as deemed necessary.

The **International Court of Justice (ICJ)** is also known as the World Court and is the principal judicial organ of the UN. ICJ's responsibilities are to adjudicate (under international law) disputes between member states and to give advisory opinions on legal issues referred to it by authorized UN organs and agencies. UN members can bring any international dispute before the Court, but all parties involved must agree to the jurisdiction of the ICJ on the dispute before the Court can take up the issue. Once a nation agrees to the handling of the dispute by the Court, it must comply with the ruling. ICJ's fifteen judges are elected by the General Assembly and the Security Council and serve nine-year terms.

The **Secretariat** is the core staff of the UN, located in New York City and in various UN offices around the world, and headed by the Secretary-General. It is charged with day-to-day administrative and substantive duties, ranging from preparing studies on the environment to running peacekeeping operations, from keeping the press and the public informed about the work of the UN to mediating international disputes. Around 16,000 employees (about 7,700 under the regular budget and the rest under special funding) from around 175 countries are employed by the UN to work as international civil servants.[5] Approximately one-third of the Secretariat works at the UN headquarters in New York City while the rest are in various parts of the world working for subsidiary bodies, with most stationed at the UN offices in Addis Ababa, Bangkok, Beirut, Geneva, Nairobi, Santiago, and Vienna.

The Secretary-General, recommended by the Security Council and elected by the GA, serves a five-year renewable term. The Secretary-General is much more than a figurehead. He initiates and supervises studies and renders opinions on global issues, sends fact-finding missions, mediates international disputes, either formally or informally, and also tries to identify and prevent potential disputes. The Secretaries-General of the UN have been:

---

5   The entire UN System, including the Secretariat, the World Bank, and the IMF, employs over 60,000 people.

- Trygve Lie (Norway) (1946–1952)
- Dag Hammarskjøld (Sweden) (1953–1961)
- U Thant (Myanmar–formerly Burma) (1961–1971)
- Kurt Waldheim (Austria) (1972–1981)
- Javier Pérez de Cuéllar (Peru) (1982–1991)
- Boutros Boutros-Ghali (Egypt) (1992–1996)
- Kofi Annan (Ghana) (1997–2006)
- Ban Ki-Moon (Republic of Korea) (2007–present)

Specialized Agencies

The UN System includes sixteen specialized agencies, some of which (e.g., Universal Postal Union) are older than the UN itself. While autonomous, most specialized agencies report to either the ECOSOC or the General Assembly, or both.

- **Food and Agriculture Organization of the UN (FAO):** Established in 1945 as the first specialized agency, FAO works around the world to fight hunger, to increase agricultural output of farmlands, forestlands, and fisheries, as well as to increase nutritional values of the produce to provide food security.
- **International Atomic Energy Agency (IAEA):** IAEA monitors the use of atomic energy and nuclear materials around the world. Its goal is to ensure that such resources are used in a safe and peaceful manner.
- **International Civil Aviation Organization (ICAO):** ICAO is the international authority responsible for setting global standards for civil aviation to ensure safety, security, and efficiency.
- **International Fund for Agricultural Development (IFAD):** IFAD works in developing countries to eliminate poverty in rural areas and help achieve higher levels of food production and nutrition consumption levels for the poor through a variety of programs as well as the provision of funding and financial services.
- **International Labour Organization (ILO):** ILO endeavors to improve working conditions, expand employment

opportunities, and achieve security and equality in the workplace around the world by setting labor standards and carrying out related programs.

- **International Maritime Organization (IMO):** IMO is the counterpart of the ICAO in sea transport, setting standards, working to make international shipping procedures safer and more efficient, and working to reduce marine pollution caused by ships.

- **International Monetary Fund (IMF):** IMF works to achieve financial stability around the world and to promote international monetary cooperation by providing a forum for cooperation and offering financial and technical advice, monitoring, and financial lending to countries facing balance-of-payment problems. It has been heavily criticized in the past for being inefficient in such assistance and in its strict monitoring and undue and excessive direction of the financial policies of countries under its assistance programs.

- **International Telecommunication Union (ITU):** ITU works with member countries in improving and standardizing telecommunications and is also responsible for coordinating the allocation of radio and TV frequencies.

- **UN Educational, Scientific and Cultural Organization (UNESCO):** UNESCO strives to promote higher education standards for all, improve scientific cooperation and knowledge, protect the cultural heritages of the world, foster freedom of press, and increase awareness of global issues.

- **UN Industrial Development Organization (UNIDO):** UNIDO helps developing countries in their industrialization efforts by providing technical expertise and training.

- **Universal Postal Union (UPU):** UPU sets standards and regulations for international postal service and cooperation between national services and offers technical assistance to its members.

- **World Bank (WB):** Originally a Bretton Woods institution, the World Bank's founding purpose was to provide funds and loans for the reconstruction and development of Europe after World War II. After realizing that goal, the World Bank today concentrates its efforts in providing grants, credit, loans, and development assistance to developing countries in order to fund educational, health, and infrastructure projects, reduce poverty, raise living standards, advance sustainable economic growth, and expand markets. The World Bank is made up of two entities: the International Bank for Reconstruction and Development (IBRD) and the International Development Association (IDA). The former focuses more on middle-income countries and the latter on the least-developed countries of the world. The World Bank lends over $20 billion to more than one hundred countries annually. The World Bank also has three affiliated agencies under its umbrella. The International Finance Corporation (IFC) works to increase private investment in less-developed regions of the world by providing to the private sector funds normally only available to national governments from the World Bank. The Multilateral Investment Guarantee Agency (MIGA) promotes foreign investment in developing countries through the guarantee of such investments against loss due to non-commercial risks in those countries. It also helps secure loans and investments for less-developed countries by providing research, financial advice, and information on investment opportunities and the creation of programs. The International Centre for the Settlement of Investment Disputes (ICSID) provides facilities for the arbitration of disputes between member countries and investors from other member countries. ICSID also engages in research and advisory activities related to international investment.

- **World Health Organization (WHO):** WHO endeavors to eradicate diseases and other global health problems, control the spread of epidemics, and provide the highest possible standard of health to all. Its work is executed through immunization campaigns and distribution of drugs, as well as health-education programs for the public and health personnel. For example, smallpox was eradicated from the world through a global campaign coordinated by WHO.
- **World Intellectual Property Organization (WIPO):** WIPO

works globally to protect intellectual property and to promote cooperation among nations with respect to copyrights, trademarks, industrial designs, and patents.

- **World Meteorological Organization (WMO):** WMO works toward more efficient sharing of meteorological observations and data, and atmospheric research.
- **World Tourism Organization (UNWTO):** UNWTO is a global forum to share knowledge related to tourism and discuss related policy issues.

Programs and Funds

The following are the specialized programs and funds within the UN System, all of which report to the GA and ECOSOC with the exception of UNRWA, which reports only to the GA:

- **Office of the UN High Commissioner for Refugees (UNHCR):** Founded in 1950, the UNHCR works with national governments and other agencies to help refugees and displaced persons who have fled war, political persecution, or human rights abuse around the world with resettlement, emergency care, and repatriation. The largest operations of the UNHCR today are assisting refugees from Afghanistan, Iraq, Sudan, and Darfur. Overall, the UNHCR works for the well-being of more than 30 million people.
- **UN Children's Fund (UNICEF):** When first established in 1946, UNICEF was a temporary relief program to help children who were victims of World War II. The Fund became a permanent organization in 1953 and is now concerned not only with providing funds and protection for child victims of war but also with the promotion of children's rights around the globe, protection of children from violence, exploitation and abuse, and the provision of food, shelter, health services, development, and education for children and their mothers.
- **The UN Conference on Trade and Development (UNCTAD):** Since its creation in 1964, UNCTAD has been working through research, technical aid, and intergovernmental exchange of ideas to help developing countries cope with

the realities of and changes in the world economic system. UNCTAD also works to integrate developing countries into this system through sustainable development efforts and increased international trade and investment. UNCTAD also cooperates with the World Trade Organization (WTO) to help developing countries export their goods through the International Trade Centre (ITC), which is the technical cooperation agency of UNCTAD and WTO.

- **UN Development Programme (UNDP):** Operating in almost 170 countries and territories, UNDP is the UN System's largest provider of grants for sustainable human development and long-term social and economic progress. The UNDP also works toward the eradication of poverty and toward increased technical cooperation. Another part of its agenda is to help countries with disaster prevention, preparedness, and management programs.

- **UN Environment Programme (UNEP):** UNEP closely monitors the environment, carries out research, publishes reports, conducts training, and helps nations protect the environment and implement environmentally sound and sustainable development policies.

- **UN Human Settlements Programme (UN-HABITAT):** UN-HABITAT provides support for people living in inadequate housing conditions and also promotes related policies.

- **UN Office on Drugs and Crime (UNODC):** UNODC works to halt the production, trafficking, and sale of illegal drugs, and to eradicate crime, terrorism, and corruption around the world. It carries out its mission through international legislation, technical assistance, crop substitution, and other rural programs.

- **UN Population Fund (UNFPA):** Originally named the United Nations Fund for Population Activities, UNFPA is the largest provider of population and reproductive assistance in the world. It works toward the reduction of infant and maternal mortality, improvement of reproductive health, increased life expectancy, and universal primary education.

- **UN Relief and Works Agency for Palestine Refugees in the Near East (UNRWA):** A temporary body whose mandate has been continuously renewed since its founding in 1949, UNRWA has provided shelter and basic services in refugee camps for millions of Palestinians. UNRWA provides Palestinian refugees with emergency relief, health, educational, and social services and coordinates international assistance to the more than four million registered Palestinian refugees in the Middle East.
- **UN World Food Programme (WFP):** WFP was founded in 1961 with the aim of providing food for the needy around the world for emergency relief and development. Today, it is the single largest donor of food aid in the world, reaching over eighty-seven million people in seventy-eight countries in 2006.

The UN System encompasses many other permanent and ad hoc committees and entities, such as the United Nations Research Institute, the United Nations International Research and Training Institute for the Advancement of Women, the United Nations Democracy Fund, and the United Nations Forum on Forests.

Related Organizations

The UN also has several related organizations:

- **International Criminal Court (ICC):** The ICC is an independent, permanent tribunal established in 2002 to prosecute individuals for alleged crimes of genocide, crimes against humanity, and war crimes. The ICC was established by the Rome Statute of the International Criminal Court, which was adopted by the General Assembly in 1998 by a vote of 120 to 7, with 21 member nations abstaining.[6] Approximately 105 countries are parties to the ICC, and some 40 countries have signed the Rome Statute but not yet ratified it. Notably, some big countries such as China, India, and the United States

---

6   The seven countries that voted against the treaty were China, Iraq, Israel, Libya, Qatar, the United States, and Yemen.

remain critical of the ICC and have so far refused to join it.

The ICC is a court of last resort, meaning it will not take action if an alleged crime is being investigated or prosecuted by a national judicial system, unless the national proceedings are not genuine. Furthermore, generally speaking, the ICC can exercise jurisdiction over an individual only if he or she is a national of a ICC member state or of a state that has accepted the jurisdiction of the ICC, the alleged crime took place within the territory of a ICC member state or in a state that accepts the jurisdiction of the ICC, or if the matter has been referred to it by the Security Council. While the ICC is an independent organization, it reports on its activities to the UN and the Security Council has certain powers relating to the ICC. The relationship between the ICC and the UN is governed by the Negotiated Relationship Agreement between the International Criminal Court and the United Nations.

- **International Seabed Authority (ISA):** The ISA was established under the United Nations Convention on the Law of the Sea. It works to organize and control activities in the international seabed and ocean floor beyond the boundaries of national jurisdiction. It is particularly focused on administering the natural resources in those areas.

- **Organisation for the Prohibition of Chemical Weapons (OPCW):** The OPCW's mandate is to implement the provisions of and monitor compliance with the Chemical Weapons Convention (CWC). The CWC is an international treaty that bans the development, production, stockpiling, transfer, and use of chemical weapons, and stipulates their timely destruction.

- **Preparatory Commission for the Comprehensive Test Ban Treaty Organization (CTBTO Prep.Com):** The Comprehensive Nuclear-Test-Ban Treaty bans all nuclear explosions (for military purposes or otherwise). The Treaty will go into force if the requisite number of signatory countries ever ratify it. If that happens, the CTBTO will be responsible for implementation and compliance matters. Until then, the CTBTO Prep.Com is acting as an interim organization, working on the establishment of a global verification regime and doing other preparatory work.

- **World Trade Organization (WTO):** The World Trade Organization's purpose is the liberalization and regulation of world trade. WTO's trade rules are the underlying trade agreements negotiated between member states. WTO serves as a forum for member nations to negotiate those agreements and settle disputes arising under them. It also administers these agreements, reviews national trade policies, and assists developing countries in trade issues through technical assistance and training. The WTO was formed in 1995 as the successor to the General Agreement on Tariffs and Trade (GATT), which was created in 1947 and operated as the de facto international trade organization until the formation of the WTO. The WTO and its underlying agreements deal not only with trade of goods but also services and trade-related intellectual property rights. WTO has over 150 member countries, which account for over 97 percent of world trade. Around thirty other countries are negotiating membership.

* * * * *

The UN accomplishes much more than any single nation could by itself, even though the UN is oftentimes criticized as ineffective. The vast organization is active in virtually every area of human life in order to better the world.

For example, the UN and its related organizations help disarmament efforts by providing a forum for negotiations, making recommendations on disarmament, setting up disarmament programs (such as those to clear landmines), and drawing up and observing compliance with multilateral treaties like the Nuclear Non-Proliferation Treaty (1968), the Comprehensive Nuclear-Test-Ban Treaty (1996), and the Ottawa Convention of 1997 on landmines. Using the good offices of the Secretary-General and other means, the UN works to settle international disputes through peacemaking. For example, the UN was instrumental in ending the Iran-Iraq war in 1988.

The UN helps in peace building in the aftermath of conflicts through development efforts and programs aimed at better governance, a stronger civil society, and rule of law. An example to this is UN's supervision of the 1989 elections in Namibia. By the authority of the Security Council, the UN also carries out peacekeeping operations around the world to maintain peace and international security by enforcing ceasefires, establishing buffer zones, and monitoring elections and peace agreements. Some peacekeeping missions are very short, such as the 1994 mission in the Aouzou Strip between Libya and Chad, which was completed in around a month, and some last years, such as the mission in Lebanon, which has been in operation since 1978. More than a hundred countries have contributed over three quarters of a million military and civilian personnel for some sixty missions.

It should be recognized that the major part of UN's work is geared toward development. Development must be understood in a broad sense, encompassing higher standards of living, better and more employment opportunities, education, the protection of women and children, economic development, raising civil awareness, eradication of poverty, fighting hunger, improvement of health, protection of the environment, promotion of human rights, population control, and good governance, among other goals.

The UN is active in all of these areas and more, by helping to raise funds, formulating policies, setting international standards, and providing personnel and technical assistance. For example, in 1948, the General Assembly adopted the Universal Declaration of Human Rights, which remains the fundamental document relating to basic rights and freedoms such as the right to life, religious and political freedom, freedom of thought, and right to education, to which all humans are entitled regardless of ethnicity, national origin, religion, or gender. The Declaration paved the way to more than eighty multilateral treaties on human rights, specifically those aimed at protecting women's and children's rights, eliminating racial discrimination, and preventing genocide. In fact, since the founding of the UN, more international law has been adopted than during all of previous history. Signing such treaties is voluntary, but once signed, a signatory becomes bound by it and the more signatories a treaty has, the stronger it becomes, pressuring non-signatories and signatories on moral and legal grounds.

In a different line of work, from the protection of Antarctica to reducing acid rain, from minimizing marine pollution to protecting the wildlife, the UN actively seeks to better the world's environment through its programs, treaties, and conventions. UN appeals raise more than $2 billion a year for emergency assistance to victims of war and natural disaster. The UN supplies food, shelter, medicine, and logistical support to the victims, most of them children, women, and the elderly, of natural disasters. The UN coordinates its response to humanitarian crises through a committee (chaired by the UN Emergency Relief Coordinator) of all of its key humanitarian bodies, as well as major nongovernmental and intergovernmental humanitarian organizations such as the Red Cross.

Cooperation in the international arena and in the UN has increased with the end of the Cold War, and the UN has devoted more effort and resources to humanitarian matters during the past decade than ever before. The traditional competition between the GA, dominated by developing nations, and the Security Council, dominated by super powers, as well as competition among those powers, has subsided, giving way to more unanimous decisions and significantly fewer vetoes in the Security Council. Nevertheless, instances of UN ineffectiveness are still a reality. Fighting still goes on around the world, and some older conflicts such as the Arab-Israeli conflict show few signs of resolution. The United States left a deep mark in people's memories by overriding the UN on the issue of Iraq.

The UN also faces a problem when nations fail to comply with treaties that are by their nature nonenforceable. Additionally, debate over the structure of the Security Council still continues.

Finally, the UN has a huge problem of debt. While the budget of the UN is minuscule compared to, for example, the world's military expenditures, many countries lag behind in their payments of UN dues. The United States is the biggest debtor, which poses a significant problem, because the United States is also the biggest contributor to the UN budget due to its large economy and high per capita income, which are the two factors used to determine UN dues.

I recommend anyone interested in Model United Nations read

further about the UN System, specifically the challenges it faces in the short and long terms.

At the time the United Nations was founded, more than seven hundred million people lived in seventy-two nonself-governing territories and eleven Trust Territories. Since then, there has been a sharp reduction in the number of people who do not live in self-governing territories and many new nations have emerged since World War II. Today, only around two million people are members of communities that do not rule themselves. In addition to the fifty-one original members, many former colonies and other nations have joined the organization.

Of course, each member nation of the UN has its own agenda, but likeminded countries with similar interests come together to form blocs in order to have more influence in the UN. There are regional blocs in the GA (see Appendix A), which are based on geographic proximity. There are also blocs such as the European Union, the North Atlantic Treaty Organization, the Non-Aligned Movement, the Association of South East Asian Nations, the Organization of American States, and the Organization of Petroleum Exporting Countries, which are examples of blocs based on shared ideological or economic interests. Members of a bloc do not always necessarily act or vote in the same way, and they can choose to act together on some issues and not on others. Some blocs may simply provide a forum to share ideas and nations may belong to several different blocs. With the end of the Cold War, blocs and bloc politics are now less important, which is likely a positive development. After all, the mission of the UN is to "conduct international relations on a cooperative, transparent and orderly basis."[7]

II. What is *Model* United Nations?

Model UN (MUN) is a simulation of the real UN in which middle school, high school, and college students participate as delegates and officials. Hundreds of thousands of students take part each year in hundreds of different conferences.

---

7   South Centre, *Reforming the United Nations: A View From the South* (Geneva, 1995), 13.

Model UN has also become a generic name, so it is often applied to conferences that include other multilateral or national bodies, such as NATO, that are not part of the UN System.

At a Model UN conference, students represent countries and play the roles of famous and not-so-famous ambassadors, diplomats, judges, and representatives in order to discuss and seek solutions to global issues. Model UN conferences tackle issues such as the environment, economic development, refugees, AIDS, conflict resolution, peace and security, human rights, food and hunger, globalization, and disarmament. During this process, participants learn about and work through negotiation and diplomacy.

Before attending conferences, students research the topics they will discuss and the countries they will represent. They also learn the rules of procedure and work on their public speaking skills. They then apply their acquired knowledge and skills when they attend conferences.

Model UN conferences began in the Northeastern United States, and at first there were only a few with limited scope. They were almost exclusively organized by university students for other university students.

Starting in the mid-1960s, Model UN conferences began to involve more university students, as well as participants from high schools and middle schools. The rest of the world began to join as well, especially in the last couple of decades, with new conferences starting out every year. Today, there are hundreds of conferences in approximately fifty countries, hosting over four hundred thousand students from thousands of high schools and universities, coming from sixth grade through graduate school.

Model UN simulations vary greatly in form and size. Some are conferences within a single school, with a few dozen participants and a single topic, lasting only one afternoon. Some larger international conferences last for five days and are attended by more than three thousand students. In between the two extremes are regional, national, and international conferences of varying sizes.

Normally, the organizers of Model UN conferences do not partake in the conference as delegates, although there are some conferences in which students from the organizing school also participate as delegates. Most conferences are organized by a single school, but there are some which are organized with the participation of multiple schools and/or other organizations.

It is noteworthy to point out that Model UN is not a direct or detailed simulation of the real UN. For example, the timeframe is radically different: issues tackled during a weekend in Model UN might consume months, sometimes years, in the actual UN. The debate is different, with Model UN being much more heated for the most part. Sometimes the issues are fictional or projections of possible future issues, or the real committee structures may be changed for Model UN purposes, to allow for formal debate. In any case, Model UN is a fun, challenging, and educational experience.

Most Model UN conferences give out awards to individual delegates or delegations in each committee and team awards to participating delegations and schools. Many delegates try their best to earn an award, while others do not care one bit about them. I do not believe you need to win an award or even try to win one to have a fruitful Model UN experience. A real *Winning Delegate* is one who successfully educates himself or herself and develops skills through participation in Model United Nations.

Model UN educates its participants in four broad categories. First, students learn core skills that they can apply to other parts of their lives: they learn to conduct research, build organizational, leadership, decision-making and problem-solving skills; they improve their command of English through reading, increasing vocabulary and formal use of spoken and written forms of the language; and they learn to speak in public, debate, negotiate, compromise, persuade, and listen.

Second, by discussing real world issues, students learn and think analytically about these issues as well as about international politics, the UN System, other international organizations, and these organizations' structures, goals, and roles in shaping international politics and global issues.

Third, by representing countries other than their own, students learn about other countries, their history, culture, geography, economics, national politics, viewpoints, policies, and concerns, and their relations with other nations.

Fourth, and most importantly—because the first three sets of skills are achievable through other means, formal schooling being the most conventional—by looking at issues through other peoples' eyes, students learn to understand and appreciate differences, become better able to do away with their prejudices and biases, become more tolerant, learn dialogue, learn the value of compromise without jeopardizing own interests, question their own beliefs and opinions, gain a broader perspective of looking at any issue, learn the value of consensus in decision-making, meet and interact with people from all sorts of backgrounds, make friends, appreciate diversity, and empathize with others.

In more than one way, Model UN prepares the individual for life through the development of these skills and provides society with more knowledgeable, open-minded, and concerned individuals.

When I began writing this book, I had a chance to ask why I participated in Model UN and what I learned from it over the years. I found two primary answers: I liked debating and public speaking, and I was interested in politics and international affairs, especially the UN System. I hope you find at least one reason too—it will make your experience that much more worthwhile and enjoyable.

CHAPTER TWO:
HOW TO PREPARE

During the summer after my freshman year in college, I was invited by my high school to give a speech to current and prospective members of the school's Model UN club. Before the meeting, I made some notes on Model UN preparation and distributed them to the students before my speech. When I began writing this book, as I was going through the many pages of Model UN-related documents I had gathered over the years, I discovered those notes, which I had called "Guidelines for Prospective Candidates." To my surprise and joy, I discovered I would probably write very similar things if I were invited to give such a speech today, and this chapter is based on those guidelines.

When you talk about preparing for a Model UN conference, it does not mean a short-term effort, like cramming for an exam, for example (which never works nearly as well as daily studying). Successful Model UN delegates are those who have prepared themselves over the years and added to that a good working knowledge of the rules, the specific topics, and, of course, experience. I advise aspiring MUNers to do the following to be better delegates.[1]

I.   General

Learn about World Affairs and Be up to Date with the News

You will know the topics to be discussed well before the conference and have a chance to read topic papers and do research, but general

---

1   Better does not only mean giving better speeches and writing better resolutions. It is a combination of many things, including, but not limited to, having more fun at a conference, being more aware of issues, and using diplomatic techniques efficiently.

knowledge attained over time will be very useful at the conference. While at the conference, you may need such knowledge to deal with a new topic in the form of a crisis, or you may want to bring in outside knowledge to make analogies and comparisons in your speeches. Furthermore, many topics have continuing developments, and you need to be up to date with these developments. To this end, I suggest you read daily newspapers—I cannot express how much you can learn just by reading, for example, *The New York Times* every day (and it is free online). Current affairs magazines help too: *The Economist*, *Time*, *Newsweek*, etc. Try to watch the news regularly on television: CNN, BBC, and the others. Finally, read books about world politics, history, economics, the environment—whatever may be useful for you to gain a better understanding of world affairs.

Advance Your Speaking and Debating Abilities

Experience does count. The more you speak in front of crowds, the more comfortable you become with the task. I recommend getting your hands on a book on public speaking to get started. As far as specific preparation techniques are concerned, as you are doing research about the issues, write short paragraphs or speech fragments. These can be a summary of an article you read or a short description of, say, the economy of a particular country. Then, read these aloud to a friend or a family member. Get feedback from these people on the content of your speech, the tone of your voice, and your body language. If no one volunteers to help, use a mirror and try to judge your own performance. If your team organizes mock debates (which it should—otherwise initiate them yourself) in preparation for a conference, take them seriously, because they are your best chance to practice your skills and get feedback from peers without the pressure of the real conference. Your teammates and chaperone are your best bets for fair and productive feedback, since they wish you to do well at the conference as much as you yourself do. Also extremely helpful is reading up on negotiation and diplomatic skills. Check your school or public library, as they should have plenty of resources.

Improve your English

Your English, even if you are a native speaker, can always improve, and the better your language skills are, the more successful you will be at Model UN. Read, read, and read. Not only for Model UN, but more importantly for life. You always need a broader vocabulary, a better knowledge of grammar, and improved writing skills.

II.   Research

You should start your research as soon as you know you are going to a conference. There is plenty to do even before you know the specific topics that you will be discussing. The earlier you start your research, the more time you will have to do it thoroughly and the more time you will have to streamline and digest all the information, write a better position paper, and come up with ideas for your speeches and resolutions. Reading through two thousand pages of research on the trip to the conference is simply not feasible. And if you realize on the bus that every page out of those two thousand refers to a key resolution that you have just then learned of and do not have a copy of, you will be very frustrated, to say the least.

Learn about the UN and Its Different Bodies

After my first few conferences, I read a book about the UN System, and at the first conference I attended after reading the book, I was much more comfortable in debate, resolution writing, and caucusing because I knew so much more about how the system worked, as well as why things worked the way they did. I suggest that aspiring MUNers get an introductory book on the UN System and read it before anything else. It is important to know precisely what it is that you are simulating. Will you necessarily need historical facts about the UN when you are at the conference? Not likely, but a general understanding of what the UN is, why it exists, and what it and its various bodies do will be important. For example, knowing the purpose, membership structure, authority, budget, key past actions, and projects of the body you are assigned to is a necessity because the policies you will help formulate will be affected by these factors. You should visit the UN and your committee's websites as well as any related websites and see what they have to reveal about themselves—they may only tell you what they do well and keep the rest to themselves, but you can count on the reliability of the information that they provide.

Learn about the Country You Will Be Representing

A good, general knowledge of your country is a must, but you need not try to learn everything about the country. Concentrate on the major things about your country, but when it comes to specifics, it will usually be enough to know only information related to your committee's topics. For example, you should have down cold the names and locations of all your country's neighbors, but you need not know about the details of your country's crop production if you are representing it in the Disarmament Committee.

By and large, smaller committees require more knowledge, because the debate is usually more substantive, the issues more specific, the delegates more experienced, and you have more opportunities to speak. It is impossible to get away with ignorance of the details of, say, the conflict in Sudan when you serve in the Security Council, but it is much easier to do so when discussing women's rights in the Human Rights Council. This is not to say that one issue is more important than the other, but in this case, for example, you may be able to hold your own with your general knowledge for the latter issue, but cannot do so with a discussion of Sudan.

Below is a list of things that you should research about your country. Use your common sense in determining what you must know, what would be good to know, and what you can forgo for your specific purposes. In addition to these, it would be good to have handy a map of the country and the region where it is located, as well as basic statistical data on the nation. The latter can be obtained from various resources: UNDP's Human Development Report, the country's government agency charged with gathering statistical data, sourcebooks, the official representation of the country nearest to your place of residence, and so on.

Geography

- Neighbors and relations with them
- Natural resources
- Topography
- Geopolitical significance and implications

Political Structure

- Type of state; type of government
- Political structure and its origins; constitution
- General policies and any particular views and policies of the current government
- Names of key people

People

- Culture and customs
- Identity: religious, ethnic, cultural, ideological
- Social development
- Religious and ethnic groups, minorities and their status

History

- General; post-World War II; recent
- Traditional allies and enemies
- Type of history—e.g., colonized, colonial power, when the country gained sovereignty, and what means were used in gaining independence (civil war, violent struggle, peaceful movement, etc.)

Economy

- General history and current situation: major products, major exports and imports, trading partners and agreements
- Welfare: per capita income, living standards
- Type of economy
- Monetary system
- Membership in economic and trade organizations (e.g., WTO, NAFTA, OPEC)

- Dependency on other countries and/or international institutions; debt
- Natural resources

International Relationships

- Formal and informal alliances; membership in international and regional organizations
- Foreign policy: basic principles; general policies (isolationist, expansionist, neutral, allied, etc.)
- Views on major world problems (the environment, human rights, disarmament, etc.)
- Status, prestige, uniqueness, role, and influence in the global arena and at the UN
- International disputes, problems, and concerns; conflicts with other countries; experience with major global problems (e.g., drug trafficking, terrorism)

Military Power

- Defense spending; strength of armed forces
- Military structure
- Dependency on other countries
- Military pacts and alliances
- Internal and external security concerns

If you are representing an organization or doing research on the particular body you are assigned to, focus on the following with respect to the entity:

- Purpose
- Membership
- History
- Structure
- Past and current projects; actions
- Influence
- Relationship of the organization to the UN

Learn about the Issues

Start your research right away, as soon as you receive the list of the topics to be discussed in your committee. The best place to begin is the topic papers that conference organizers send you. These will usually give you a good overview of the topic and a sense of what you should be looking for. If the organizers send no such papers or you do not receive them within a reasonable time before the conference, start without them.

Using published sources and the Internet, learn about the historical and geopolitical background to the topics as well as the current situation. Study the map of the region; it will make things clearer as you progress through your research.

In addition to background research, you should find, read, and copy available treaties, conventions, agreements, UN resolutions, reports, and other relevant documents that specifically pertain to the assigned issue.

At the end of your research, you should have a good grasp of the issue and be able to:

- Describe the issue in a few sentences
- Identify the parties involved and concerned
- Explain how it concerns or affects your nation and your nation's viewpoint
- Know other relevant countries' positions on the issue

Finding information on your country's viewpoint on an issue is sometimes clear-cut, but information is not always readily available. Nevertheless, you can deduce a lot from your nation's general policy and interests, its alliances, past voting record, and actions on the same or similar issues. In any case, almost no country has a black-and-white point of view on any issue. A country's stance on an issue is oftentimes dynamic and sometimes undefined. National policies are constantly altered by factors such as changes in government, the need for compromise due to other issues, the current world situation, and public perception.

Speeches given by the leaders and representatives of your country in the recent past are primary sources and will help you greatly. UN voting records are also good indicators of where a country is likely to stand on a certain matter. But be aware that you do not have the time at the conference that countries have in the real world to devote to these issues. You cannot wait for too long before you take a stance on an issue, otherwise you will leave the impression that you have not done your homework. Having no policy at all is worse than having a somewhat unrealistic one. Having said that, when you must speculate on your country's policy, stick to facts you know, but also think analytically before and during the conference, and do not be afraid to formulate a new policy if you think it proper.

Researching the view points of other countries and blocs on an issue is more difficult as well as time consuming. Speaking realistically, you will not have too much time to spend on this task. Work strategically. Learn about the policies of the most relevant parties to an issue and major players as well as general bloc positions when applicable. Also, if there are key resolutions on the topic, look at the voting records on those resolutions. Then pay attention during debate, especially opening speeches, and you will get a good idea as to where each country stands. You should do this even if you have done research on everyone's position, because not everyone will be on-policy at the conference.

When you are finished with your research, I suggest making a cheat sheet of important facts about your assigned country, the body in which you will be representing your country, and the issues to be discussed. The sheet could include your country's neighbors, a list of the members of the committee, and a list of the major points about the issue. This list will come in handy during the conference when making speeches and writing resolutions.

Topic Papers

Several weeks prior to the conference, the organizers will probably send your school a summary of each topic. These summaries, called topic papers, will have background information on the subject matter, as well as a short synopsis of the positions of the bloc and of certain countries. Topic papers will usually also lay out the expectations of the session chair in terms of debate and resolution writing at the conference. If well researched and well written, topic papers are a delegate's best starting place to prepare for the conference. As well as giving you a general understanding of the topic in a text of manageable length, the paper's bibliography will guide you in the right direction for further research.

I have read some excellent topic papers and some really poor ones: their quality was always a good indication of what the committee was going to be like. Good chairs and good staffs write good topic papers, and a good Secretariat edits them well. I believe that the quality of its topic papers shows the respect that a conference has for its participants.

Position Papers (Background Paper/Policy Statements)

Most conferences these days require delegates to write a few paragraphs or pages on their delegation's position on the agenda topics before the conference. The reasons for this are:

First, conference organizers want the delegates to spend at least some time researching and thinking about the topics before they come to the conference—this raises the level of debate at the conference.

Second, some conferences use these papers in determining awards. Truth be told, they do not carry a heavy weight but a well-written position paper (or simply one that was written at all) can be a tiebreaker. Even so, most students do not write position papers ahead of time or at all unless forced by their faculty advisor or team leader. I suggest you write a position paper, even if it is not required. Position papers can come in handy during the conference and they usually provide a good basis for opening speeches, that is, your first speech on a topic in which you outline your position on the issue.

Some conferences require position papers to include not only information about the nation's stance on the issues but also basic information, such as geography, economy, political structure, its role in the UN, etc., on the nation itself. If it is not required, do not spend time summarizing the basics. Your paper also need not repeat or summarize the issue—the organizers already know it. What you need is to-the-point information about what your country thinks about the issue, why it thinks so, how it is affected by the issue, its relations with involved parties, and your suggestions for a solution. If you will be representing an organization or an individual rather than a country, the logic behind your position papers will be the same.

Speech Outlines

I have never believed in writing speeches before or during the conference, because I do not like to read from a written text and committee dynamics make it practically impossible to predict what path the debate will follow. Nevertheless, I still believe that making a list of major points you know you will make at some point during debate can be helpful. However, some people find it a good idea to write or outline speeches they know they will deliver, such as a speech on setting the agenda or the opening speech on an issue.

Draft Resolutions

I will discuss resolutions and draft resolutions in Chapter Six, but a few words about them are necessary here. Some conferences accept draft resolutions on the committee topics prior to the conference, but most do not. Whatever the conference policy, it is extremely important at least to think about ideas for a resolution and to write them down in idea or clause form. You will be able to draw on this work for your speeches and when writing resolutions with other delegates during the conference.

Learn the Rules of Procedure

Most rules of procedure stay the same from conference to conference, at least in the same country or continent, although there is occasionally some variation. All of Chapter Three will be devoted to these rules.

I have tried to be as clear as possible when explaining the rules; however, to the beginner, they may be very confusing as they are quite complex. A good grasp of the rules of procedure comes only with committee experience. Nevertheless, it is a good idea to read and to try to understand the rules before the conference. The organizers will probably send your team a copy of the rules prior to the conference, and many conferences nowadays make their rules available online.

Inexperienced delegates should seek the help of more

experienced delegates in understanding the rules. Even if you have been to conferences before, you should review the rules, as it is easy to forget them and they may vary from conference to conference and even from one year to the next at the same conference. When you conduct mock debates with your team, have someone who knows the rules well chair the session and stick to the rules as if you were at the conference. It is also a good idea to make yourself a cheat sheet of the rules, which you can keep with you during the conference. The best Model UN delegates know the rules of procedure cold.

III.   Preparing as a Group

It is imperative that Model UN teams meet regularly during preparations for a conference. Team members must get to know each other in order to build a team spirit and identity, and in order to decide on a team strategy for the conference. Such meetings are forums for members to learn from one another's research, to run through debate strategies and resolution writing, and to practice together using the rules of procedure.

Research

Since most members of a team will be doing much of the same research—for example, research that is not specific to an issue—it is a good idea to share this work. Each person on the delegation can be assigned a part of the research, such as the founding of the UN or the strength of the armed forces of the country to be represented, with each person writing a page-long summary of the most important points relating to his or her portion of the research. This way, you would have a full research on the organization and your assigned country, and everyone would have more time to spend on researching their specific topics.

This system would also assure that the research gets done and gets done on time. While an individual delegate may be satisfied with less than thorough research on the country and may put it off until the last minute, the sense of responsibility to his or her teammates will likely be sufficient pressure to do a good job. By the same logic, if you work with a partner in your committee, divide up the work fairly and efficiently so that you can get more done.

Advance cooperative work on topics is less feasible but not altogether impossible. Topics can overlap between committees, so look at the topics of the other committees and see if you can work and share research with your teammates. Also, ask your teammates if they have anything that may be useful for you. The same topics get used over and over from conference to conference, and the chances are there will be someone on your team who has done research in previous years on the same or a very similar topic. Many Model UN clubs also maintain a small library of resources. Ask your faculty advisor or whoever is in charge of the team if the club has any materials that you may use.

Team Identity and Strategy

Just knowing about the issues and the rules of procedure is not enough at the conference. You may be the representative of country X in your committee, but you are also a team member of the delegation of country X from school Y, and when sessions are over at the end of the day, you want to have made a good impression about both your team and your country.

To accomplish this, two things are necessary: you, as the individual, must identify yourself with your country and your team, and your team should act like a team. That is, all members of the delegation must be geared toward the same goals and represent the assigned country or countries with similar strategies. Of course, each person has a different style of debate and set of skills, but team play is still possible with different personalities. For example, some military schools wear their uniforms on the first and last day of the conference to establish and distinguish themselves as a team. If everyone on your team wears a pin of the flag of your assigned country, it will have a similar effect. However, note that many conferences prohibit the wearing of any national or political symbols.

It is also important to remember that each issue and committee at the conference plays only a partial role in the overall picture and foreign policy of your country. Only the composite of the positions of individual delegates on the various issues makes sense as the policy and position of a delegation. Determining an overall strategy and goal involves factors such as the country assignment, the people on your team, and the type of conference. For example, it is possible for delegates to be more confrontational and less compromising when representing a superpower than when representing a small island state. You will need to decide on the following things:

- The general and specific goals of the delegation
- The general attitude of the team (aggressive, neutral, etc.)
- What you can and cannot compromise on
- Who your likely allies, co-workers and adversaries will be

Mock Debates

Holding mock debate sessions prior to the conference is essential in delegate preparation. These debates allow delegates to improve their public speaking skills, expand and improve their knowledge of the rules of procedure, and become more comfortable at role playing. Mock debates are the best forum to get objective and constructive feedback from peers and chaperons. You can debate real issues or come up with imaginative ones to make the experience more fun, but in any case, take the exercise seriously, and you will benefit from it greatly.

IV. How and Where to Conduct Your Research

I realize that it is tempting to turn to the Internet to do all your research, and I fully appreciate the fact that the Internet offers a wide variety of resources on every topic. A good Internet research may greatly reduce the need to do traditional research. Be careful, however, especially when it comes to controversial topics such as a border dispute. You may find a lot of out-of-date, inaccurate, biased, provocative, untruthful, and even offensive websites. This is due to the mostly unregulated nature of the Internet. Published resources, in general, are more reliable and comprehensive. Use common sense; it is relatively easy to distinguish between a respectable organization's website and one prepared by a sympathizer of an oppressive regime.

Whatever the topic, do thorough research on the historical background of the subject matter. You do not need to remember every detail, but you should be very much aware of major events, terms, and names. If your resources refer to important past resolutions or other documents, find them on the relevant organization's website and read them. I also find it useful at least to skim through other resolutions and documents. You can use the information you obtain both in making speeches and in writing resolutions. The UN often repeats itself in subsequent resolutions on a single topic, and there is no reason you cannot do the same or at least be inspired by previous resolutions.

Almost every country and each state in the Unites States has UN depository libraries, which offer thousands of books and other UN publications, including resolutions that are available to the general public. A full list of UN Depositories can be found at http://www.un.org/depts/dhl/deplib/countries.

Embassies, Consulates, and Other People and Places to Contact

Representations of countries are generally very happy to help MUNers and can provide current and hard-to-find information. Contact the embassy, nearest consulate, or trade delegation for the country you will be representing. Do it as early as possible, because the staff there may be busy. But, when they do have time for you, they can be great sources for information that you cannot find elsewhere. You can communicate with them by e-mail, fax, or mail, or conduct a mission trip as a team to the representation. Many member nations also have home pages for their permanent missions, and these pages usually contain valuable resources. See the next section for web addresses that will direct you to the right contact information.

You can also reach out to teachers, school or public librarians, scientists, experts, businessmen, NGOs, government agencies, interest groups, and ministries of foreign affairs to get guidance on your research.

V.   Resources

While the following list is by no means exhaustive, the resources I list below are good places to use for research during your conference preparations.

Bookstores and Publishers

- UN publications website at https://unp.un.org. Online and published resources, books, reports of UN bodies, posters, stamps, and more as well as an order form.
- The United Nations Information Centres (UNICs) offer UN documents for free. You need to know the document number in order to place an order—use the Internet to find the numbers. To locate the UNIC nearest to you, go to http://www.un.org/aroundworld/unics/english/about.htm.
- United Nations Bookshop. Publications, souvenirs and more. Located in the Visitors Lobby of the UN building at 46th Street and 1st Avenue, New York, NY 10017, USA; tel: +1 (212) 963-7680; bookshop@un.org; https://unp.un.org/bookshop.
- The United Nations Association of the United States of America (UNA-USA) publishes UN and Model UN-related books and other publications, and also has a wide variety of Model UN-related information on its website at http://www.unausa.org.

Books and Other Publications

- *Charter of the United Nations.* Available at public libraries, as well as on the UN website.
- *Annual Report of the Secretary-General on the Work of the Organization.* Submitted each year by the Secretary-General to the General Assembly, the report discusses the UN's work in the past year. Published by the UN and available for free on the UN website.
- *Index to Proceedings of the General Assembly: Index to Speeches.* Reference information on all speeches delivered before the GA. Published by the UN.
- *Index to Proceedings of the General Assembly: Subject Index.* Reference information on meetings, membership in subsidiary bodies, agendas, reports, resolutions, decisions, and voting. Published by the UN.
- *Index to Proceedings of the Security Council.* Reference

information on speeches, voting records, resolutions, and other documents. Published by the UN.

- *CIA World Factbook.* Basic information and statistics on countries of the world. Available for purchase at http://bookstore.gpo.gov or free online at http://www.cia.gov. Updated annually.
- *Human Development Report.* Published annually by the UNDP. Compares many social and economic indicators for the world's nations. Available for purchase or free download at http://www.undp.org.
- *World Statistics Pocketbook.* More than fifty economic, social, and environmental indicators for over 200 countries and areas. Published by the UN.

News Resources

- BBC News. The website of the British Broadcasting Corporation, the world's largest broadcasting corporation. http://news.bbc.co.uk
- *The Economist.* British weekly magazine with articles on world news, economics, and politics. http://www.economist.co.uk
- *Foreign Affairs.* Published six times a year by the Council on Foreign Relations. Includes articles by experts on many international relations and foreign policy matters. http://www.foreignaffairs.org
- *Foreign Policy.* Magazine of international affairs, global politics, and economics. http://www.foreignpolicy.com
- *The International Herald Tribune.* Published by *The New York Times*, this is the premier international daily newspaper in English. http://www.iht.com
- *The New York Times.* Arguably the best daily newspaper in the United States. http://www.nytimes.com
- *Reuters.* One of the world's leading providers of news and financial information.

http://www.reuters.com

- *UN Wire.* Daily electronic newsletter of the UN Foundation covering UN-related topics with many links.
  http://www.unwire.org
- *United Nations Chronicle.* Quarterly magazine published by the UN. Reports on the work of the UN and its agencies.
  http://www.un.org/Pubs/chronicle
- *United Nations News.* UN-related news from the official news service of the UN.
  http://www.un.org/news
- *The Washington Post.* Daily newspaper with a more conservative view than *The New York Times.*
  http://www.washingtonpost.com

Web Resources

United Nations System

- United Nations Homepage. The best place to begin your research. Thousands of resolutions and documents, background information on UN bodies and issues, and many links.
  http://www.un.org
- UN Documentation Centre. Resolutions, maps, and other documents.
  http://www.un.org/documents
- UN Member States. List of UN members and other information on members and observers.
  http://www.un.org/members
- UN Protocol and Liaison Service. Contact information for member states and observers, lists of heads of state, heads of government and ministers of foreign affairs for each member, and other useful information about members and observers.
  http://www.un.int/protocol
- UN System—"Official Web Site Locator for the UN System of Organizations." Information on the UN System, links to and email addresses for organizations within the system.
  http://www.unsystem.org
- UN System Pathfinder. Suggested publications and links to

Internet resources.
http://www.un.org/Depts/dhl/pathfind/frame/start.htm

Model United Nations

- United Nations Cyberschoolbus Model UN site. Part of the UN's "Global Teaching and Learning Project." Information on current world affairs and Model UN for the elementary and secondary school levels.
  http://cyberschoolbus.un.org/modelun

Intergovernmental Organizations

- African Union (AU)
  http://www.africa-union.org
- African, Caribbean and Pacific Group of States (ACP)
  http://www.acpsec.org
- Association of Caribbean States (ACS)
  http://www.acs-aec.org
- Association of Southeast Asian Nations (ASEAN)
  http://www.aseansec.org
- Caribbean Community (CARICOM)
  http://www.caricom.org
- The Commonwealth
  http://www.thecommonwealth.org
- Council of Europe (CoE)
  http://www.coe.int
- European Union (EU)
  http://www.europa.eu
- Group of 77 (G77)
  http://www.g77.org
- International Criminal Police Organization (INTERPOL)
  http://www.interpol.int
- North Atlantic Treaty Organization (NATO)
  http://www.nato.int
- Organisation for Economic Co-operation and Development (OECD)
  http://www.oecd.org

- Organization of American States (OAS)
  http://www.oas.org
- Western European Union (WEU)
  http://www.weu.int
- World Trade Organization (WTO)
  http://www.wto.org

Other

- EmbassyWorld.com. Contact information for embassies and consulates around the globe.
  http://www.embassyworld.com
- The Global Policy Forum. Monitors the work of the UN.
  http://www.globalpolicy.org
- International Crisis Group. Analyses of current crises in the world.
  http://www.crisisgroup.org
- United Nations Foundation. Works to improve the work in the UN by raising funds and increasing public awareness for the organization.
  http://www.unfoundation.org
- The United Nations Intellectual History Project. Books and oral histories on the UN, its organizations and their work.
  http://www.unhistory.org

CHAPTER THREE:
RULES OF PROCEDURE

I. Overview

Most rules of procedure stay the same around the world, but some occasionally differ depending on the country and the conference. Furthermore, different committees within the same conference may have slightly different rules. For example, one body may operate on unanimous decision-making whereas another may use simple majority. However, the basic idea behind any set of Model UN rules is the same. They are essentially adapted from the rules of procedure used by the United Nations and modified to suit the needs of Model UN conferences. Some conferences use *Robert's Rules of Parliamentary Procedure* as the basis for or to supplement their own rules.

Generally, the specific rules of procedure of a conference, along with the rulings of the Secretary-General, Secretariat, and the chairing staff, take precedence over the UN Charter and *Robert's Rules*. Some conferences also allow their committees to adopt new rules to supplement the existing ones (but not in any way to amend or supersede them). When you get your delegate guide, read, understand, and accept the rules as they are in the guide, leaving your preconceptions behind. Challenging the rules or using them in a different fashion than allowed will only hurt your experience and everyone else's.

This chapter is devoted to introducing and explaining rules and procedures most commonly used at conferences around the world. I have included the variations to the extent practicable. Where there are multiple applications or interpretations of a rule, I have explained the most common ones. However, it is practically impossible to include every variation of the rules, and when you attend a conference, you may see different applications of certain rules than the ones described here or see rules not covered here.

You will find that this chapter, by and large, only deals with what the rules are, how they are used, and occasionally with why they exist and how they are used. Tips and suggestions on how to work with the rules are included in Chapter Five: The Committee.

Participants

Delegates

Each country or entity represented in a body of the conference is called a delegation. This should not be confused with the term delegation as used to refer to the whole team from a single school or all the participants representing the same country at the conference. Accordingly, individual participants are called delegates. It is also acceptable to refer to delegates as representatives. Most simulations at the conference will be committees with countries as representatives, but there are also nonconventional committees in which delegates represent individuals (such as the national cabinet of a country) or do not represent anyone (such as press corps). A country can be represented by a single delegate or multiple delegates in each committee, but I personally have never seen more than three delegates representing a single country in a committee.

Observers

Each delegation in a committee typically represents a member state, whether as a direct simulation of the real-life UN committee or in an imaginary setup. These delegations, as in the real world, will have the right to express their opinions on issues, make points or motions, and vote (unless it is a non-voting body). In addition, there may be observer nations or delegations. These exist in real international bodies and are typically endowed with all rights and privileges of full delegations save the right to vote, although depending on the specific conference and nature of the observer, additional rights may be granted or taken away from these delegations. For example, while the General Assembly gives every right but voting rights to the Holy See as an observer, a press corps observer may be allowed only to observe the proceedings and take notes and pictures. Observers may also be prohibited from making or seconding certain motions such as a motion to adjourn, motion to close debate, or motion to question competence. Larger conferences are more likely to have observers, especially in the General Assembly (as is the case in the real UN). For a list of observers, see Appendix A.

Staff Members

There are two main groups of staff members: the Secretariat and the chairing staff. These officers will not have the right to vote on any issue, substantive or procedural. The Secretariat (everyone from the Secretary-General to administrative members) is in charge of running the conference and administrative issues. The chairing staff, otherwise known as the dais, of a specific committee will have various titles, depending on the conference and committee, and is in charge of running that committee's proceedings. For the purposes of this chapter, I will refer to the person managing the proceedings by the generic term "chair."

II.   Rules of Procedure

Language

While the UN has six official languages[1] (Arabic, Chinese, English, French, Russian, and Spanish), almost all Model UN conferences use English as the official and working language of the conference. However, there are also some non-English speaking and bilingual conferences around the world. Many conferences allow delegates to use other languages when making a speech or to distribute written material in another language but require that they provide an

---

1   English and French are the working languages of the UN Secretariat. In addition to the six official languages, Russian is also a working language in the GA. English, French, and Spanish are the working languages of ECOSOC.

English translation. Such conferences will typically count both the time required for the translation and the original speech against the speakers' regular speaking time. In any case, it is rare that anyone will deliver a speech in a language other than the official language of the conference.

When I was an undergraduate MUNer at Yale, upon request of the committee or the chair's discretion, we brought into committees special delegates, who were staff members acting as ambassadors or experts on the issue, some of whom would speak in a foreign language while the Secretariat provided simultaneous translation into English. This system not only made the experience more realistic but also provided a more lively and entertaining environment for the participants. Some conferences allow delegates to make a motion to request a representative from a nation or international organization (the rules will typically require that topic being discussed involve that nation or international organization) to join the proceedings either for a question and answer session or with debating privileges. If the motion passes, the Secretariat will provide the requested representative.

Quorum

A quorum is the minimum number of delegates that must be present in the chamber for a committee to start proceedings. Some conferences or committees may have no quorum requirement. Others may have relatively low ones, such as one-fifth of the members; yet others may have high quorum requirements, such as two-thirds, or the presence of all members (higher quorum requirements are generally seen in smaller committees, such as the Security Council). The presence of a quorum is generally assumed unless challenged. Quorum may cease to exist during proceedings, but this will not typically stop the proceedings. However, for a substantive question to be put to a vote, the presence of a quorum will typically be required, and such quorum may be different from the quorum required for the deliberations.

Roll Call

Roll call is always the first thing on the agenda at the opening of each session. It simply means that a staff member goes through an alphabetical list of all delegations and notes whether they are present in the chamber. It is sufficient to simply say "present" (or "here") when your delegation's name is called. If you identify yourself as "present and voting," that means you intend not to and will not be allowed to abstain on substantive matters. If a delegation comes in after roll call, the dais may simply make a note of it, which is typical in small committees, or ask that such delegation send a note to the dais stating that they are now present. At most conferences, a delegation that is not officially present will not be recognized for any purpose while some conferences will recognize the delegation for speeches and motions but will not permit it to vote.

Placards

Each delegation represented in a committee will have a placard bearing the name of the country or organization they represent. When a delegate wishes to be recognized by the chair for any purpose, he or she needs to raise this placard.

Agenda

The agenda of a committee is composed of the topics to be discussed by the body over the course of the conference. Some conferences have only a single topic in each committee but most will assign multiple topics to its committees. When there are multiple topics, the order of topics to be discussed may be predetermined by the Secretariat or the chair, but usually the committee will be asked to order its own topics.

Provisional Agenda

These are the topics of a body as predetermined by the Secretariat. They are not necessarily listed in any order but some conferences order them according to a "provisional priority."

Adoption (Establishment) of the Agenda

The adoption of the agenda is usually the first thing a committee does after roll call. It means organizing the provisional agenda into the order in which items will be discussed. A temporary speakers' list will be established or the chair may simply call on delegates to make speeches, much like in a moderated caucus (see below). Speakers can propose the order in which they would like the agenda topics to be discussed and their reasons for the order they propose, or they can speak in favor or against an order proposed by another speaker. When the chair feels that ample debate and caucusing have taken place, he or she will entertain a motion to adopt the agenda in a particular order. Some conferences require that all topics be ordered when adopting the agenda, while others are satisfied with choosing only the first topic to be discussed and then adopting new topics as they exhaust previous ones. The committee then votes either on the first proposed order without hearing any other ones or in order of proposing after all order proposals have been made. In any case, the first proposal to be adopted will end debate on the adoption of the agenda, and the committee will take on the first topic and begin debating it. A simple majority is the typical requirement for adoption of an agenda, although other majority and at times plurality variations are used too. Adoption of the agenda is a procedural issue and thus yields and caucuses (see below) are prohibited in most conferences.

Change of the Agenda

This is the reordering of topics and can usually only be done after a substantive topic has been successfully closed or tabled. It usually requires a simple majority to pass, and a limited number of speeches for and against the motion will typically be allowed. Some conferences allow open debate on the motion.

Addition to the Agenda

Most conferences allow the addition of topics that are not part of the provisional agenda. These are sometimes called "supplementary items." However, allowing such a motion is usually at the discretion of the chair, and chairs are generally unwilling to entertain such motions unless the motion is aimed at adding a crisis topic introduced by the Secretariat or rewording or amending an existing topic to clarify it, or expand or narrow its focus. A motion to add to the agenda is generally entertained only after a substantive topic has been successfully closed or tabled. It usually requires a simple majority to pass, and speeches for and against will typically be allowed.

Some conferences also allow supplementary item proposals to be made by delegations prior to the conference. Proposals must typically be submitted along with an explanatory memorandum and, if possible, basic documents and/or a draft resolution on the topic. Conferences that allow such proposals will either allow the Secretariat to decide whether to add the proposed topic to the agenda or have the committee decide on its addition at the conference.

Deliberations (Debate)

Formal Debate

Formal debate is normally conducted according to a speakers' list and consists of debate on the topic on the table and any related substantive motions under consideration (i.e., resolutions and amendments). While most conferences allow joint debate on a topic and all related substantive motions, some conferences will allocate separate times to specific substantive motions and the topic itself. However, some conferences do not use speakers' lists, and formal debate in those conferences resembles moderated caucus (see below).

Caucus

Caucus, otherwise known as un-moderated caucus, lobbying, or consultative session, takes place by interrupting formal debate for a short time period, usually five to twenty minutes. This allows delegates to discuss the issues informally by moving around the chamber and forming small discussion groups. Entertaining a motion for caucus is at the discretion of the chair, and if entertained, it usually requires a simple majority to pass, with no speeches for or against it. Motions for caucus are not in order during voting procedure.

Moderated Caucus

Sometimes called suspension of the rules or informal session, moderated caucus allows quick discussion of issues by moving the body into informal debate. Unlike regular caucus, delegates are required to remain in their seats and refrain from speaking without being recognized. Instead of using the speakers' list, the chair calls on delegates to make speeches from among those who express the desire to speak by raising their placards to make speeches.

Moderated caucus is an excellent tool for discussing amendments or crisis situations, and the purpose of the moderated caucus is usually determined before suspending the rules in an effort to ensure that speeches pertain to the purpose of the motion. A motion for moderated caucus is in order only during formal debate.

Some conferences use the moderated caucus method of debate with all other rules intact as their regular formal debate format. I have observed that this speakers' list-free method requires a much more attentive chairing staff, who usually have to keep a list of speeches to ensure fairness in recognizing delegates. Even so, especially in large committees, it usually gives delegations a better chance of getting on the podium, provided the chair is doing his or her job properly. Good chairs will know whom to call on and when, if they follow the proceedings and caucuses closely. Where moderated caucus is used as the regular method of formal debate, conference rules may set overall time limits, either on a topic as a whole or on each substantive motion. These time limits may also divide the debate into for and against blocks (called closed debate). For example, if thirty minutes of speaking time is set on a resolution, this can be divided into fifteen minutes of "for" time and fifteen minutes of "against" time, or simply thirty minutes of open debate. The time limits may be extended, although maximum time limits are usually set, such as three hours on each resolution.

Speakers' List

The speakers' list determines the order of speeches made by delegations during formal debate. Before formal debate on a question begins, the chair will typically form the initial list by asking delegations to raise their placards and arranging them into a speaking order. This order usually seems to be random but experienced chairs will know to balance the representation of different viewpoints, whenever these are predictable. After the initial drawing of the speakers' list, delegations are usually asked to submit in writing their requests to be placed on the list. Delegations are normally not permitted to be on the speakers' list more than once at any given time. The expiration of the speakers' list usually means the automatic closure of debate and moving into voting procedure.

Closure and Reopening of Speakers' List

At any time during formal debate, it is possible to close the speakers' list by vote of the committee, which means no delegates may be added to the list after adoption of the motion to close. The list may later be reopened provided that at least one speaker remains on the list at the time the motion to reopen is made. Both motions to close and to reopen the list are ordinarily debatable. The motion to close is customarily harder to pass under the rules and rarely requires less than a two-thirds majority, whereas a simple majority will typically suffice to reopen the list.

Speeches

Most conferences establish time limits for speeches, although some conferences leave the time allocated for a speech up to the chair's discretion. Conferences that have no set time limits will typically permit the chairing staff to set time limits as they see necessary. Some conferences also allow the chairing staff to limit the number of times a delegate is permitted to speak on a particular topic. Time limits on speeches are generally a few minutes, which is long enough to get a few main points across but too short to deal with all issues and data. Time limits are easy to change, either by chair discretion (experienced chairs will know when and how to adjust time limits before anyone complains) or by a simple majority vote. Some conferences allow their committees to vote to allow a particular speaker speak for longer than the established time limit, but this will typically be allowed once per speaker during the conference (or topic).

Whether in formal debate or moderated caucus, no delegate may speak prior to being recognized by the chair, even if he or she is next on the speakers' list and there are no other points or motions on the floor. Once recognized, depending on the setup of the body and the room, and to an extent the discretion of the chair, the representative may go up to the podium, stand up in place, or remain seated to deliver his or her speech. It is imperative that speeches pertain to the topic on the floor; otherwise the chair will call the speaker to order.

Yields and Comments

At the end of his or her speech, a speaker can typically do one of four things:
1. Yield to another delegate
2. Yield to points of information
3. Yield to the chair
4. Not yield at all

Some conferences require that an intention to yield be made prior to beginning a speech. I find such a rule counterintuitive as well as counterproductive. Many factors may make a delegate decide what to do with his or her time: a signal from a fellow delegate, something he or she decides to add to or subtract from his or her speech as it is being delivered, or simply the reaction of other delegates. If you yield before a speech, you cannot change your mind later on. I have always preferred to let delegates make their yields at any time during the speech.

Yielding to Another Delegate

It is possible for a recognized speaker to yield remaining or even all speaking time to another delegate. I do not know of any conference that allows double yields, that is, when a delegate who has been yielded to yields to a third delegate or yields back to the original speaker.

The reasons to yield to a fellow delegate may vary. You may be working on a resolution or amendment with someone, and each of you may want to talk about different aspects of it, depending on your contribution to or expertise, and thus share a speech. Sometimes, it is effective to share time with a country that is in a different political, regional, or religious bloc in order to attract wider support for what you have to say.

Yielding to Points of Information

Points of information are questions asked of a speaker at the end of his or her speech (this is discussed in more detail below). Only delegates who have not been yielded to may yield to points of information. There are three ways time may be allocated to points of information:

1. Both the questions and the answers count against the speakers' time

2. Only the answers but not the questions count against the time limit

3. The rules or the chair establish an additional time limit for points of information and/or determine the number of questions that may be asked.

The last method is obviously the most advantageous to speakers but is rarely used. When I used to chair committees, I always preferred to use the second method, because I believe counting the time spent asking the questions (and they almost always needs repeating) against the speakers' time limit is unfair to the speaker. Most conference rules will not clarify the procedure, and chairs will generally be uncertain about what they should and wish to do. (It's annoying.) It is a good idea early on in the conference to rise to a point of parliamentary inquiry (see below) and ask the chair to clarify the method to be used.

Yielding to the Dais

Speakers may yield their remaining time to the chair, once they complete their speech. Even if the speaker has no time left, it is, at least in my opinion, still technically valid to yield to the chair. Not doing so should result in conceding to comments (discussed below), if they are permitted. It is neither necessary nor technically possible for yielded delegates to yield to the chair in anticipation of avoiding comments, as such comments are customarily allowed only after speeches made by the original speaker.

No Yields

If a speaker concludes his or her remarks and simply takes his or her seat, comments will be in order (if allowed by the rules), provided the speaker was not yielded to. However, there are two viewpoints on what happens if the speaker has already exhausted his or her time limit completely at the time he or she sits down without yielding. One point of view is that the full use of a time limit constitutes, in and of itself, an unstated declaration by the speaker that he or she wishes no one else to have a say, including comments, during the time he or she has the floor. Thus, there is no need to explicitly declare a yield. While I understand the reasoning behind this, I am still a believer of the opposing point of view, which says that it is irrelevant how much or whether all of the speaking time has been used and that the speaker is still technically required to yield (in any way he or she wishes) to prevent comments. In this view, whether there is time available to execute the yield is irrelevant. On a practical level, I also find this easier to apply when chairing: Forget about what the stopwatch says—if the speaker does not yield, someone can get up there and make a comment.

Comments

If a speaker who has not been yielded time fails to make a yield at the end of his or her remarks, most conferences allow comments to be made by other delegates. Comments are usually limited to one or two delegates after each speech and have very short time limits, usually twenty to thirty seconds for each comment, making sure it remains a comment and does not become another speech. Comments must pertain to the previous speech and commenting on another comment is out of order.

Point of Information

A point of information is a question on the issue at hand or the speech just delivered by the speaker, except speeches on procedural matters. The question can ask the speaker to clarify a point made in his or her speech or can be a general question about the topic. It is out of order to make a comment when recognized to make a point of information. It is also out of order to ask dilatory or irrelevant questions.

Even if a delegate does not yield time when finished with his or her remarks (in which case comments are normally in order), another delegate may rise to a point of information and the speaker will, in most conferences, be allowed to accept the point of information. This is another gray area of rules of procedure. If and when there are multiple motions on the floor, the chair will call on a delegate to make his or her motion, and if it warrants consideration, then should ask if there are preceding motions on the floor before executing the motion or putting it to vote. In the case of non-yield, though, it is sometimes not possible to follow this conventional method: after a non-yield, a motion to comment is automatically in order unless there is a preceding motion. Comments are generally not listed in orders of precedence because of their narrow and specific use. It is safe to say that since comments are a natural consequence to non-yields, they will precede points of information but will be preceded by non-exclusionary parliamentary points or motions, namely, a point of order, appeal, point of personal privilege, point of parliamentary inquiry, and right of reply. Even if such motions are executed, comments can still be made afterwards. What I mean by gray area is the case of the first point to be recognized being a request for a point of information and the chair asking the body if there are preceding points or motions. If another delegate has a motion to comment, does it precede the point of information? I believe it does, because rising to a point of information after a non-yield carries with it the uncertain expectation that the delegate will accept it, but a comment after a yield is the natural consequence. However, some chairs ask the delegate anyway, showing flexibility in giving them the benefit of the doubt that they did not intentionally fail to yield and may just have forgotten to do so.

One last comment about points of information: The speaker can refuse to answer any of them and can also decide to stop accepting them completely.

Right of Reply

A delegate who feels that a remark made by another delegate has impugned his or her personal or national integrity may request in writing, or by a motion immediately after the speech has been completed, a right of reply. The reply, when granted, must pertain only to the alleged offensive remark and nothing else. A right of reply is essentially a defensive tool and should be used as such, since no right of reply to a right of reply can be granted. Such impunity means that the right of reply must be used with special care. It is very rare that such a request is made, as even the most excited delegates usually know their limits. It is even rarer that the request is granted—chairs are usually worried that the right of reply will be more offensive than the original remark and therefore would rather let the original remark stand than take the risk of having one more angry delegate.

Lay on the Table (Adjournment or Postponement of Debate)

A successful motion to lay the current topic or substantive motion on the table means the suspension of all debate on that topic or motion until it is taken from the table again, if that happens at all. The motion is usually debatable and typically requires a simple majority to pass. It can be made at anytime during formal debate on the topic (few conferences allow it under other circumstances) and cannot interrupt a speech. Some conferences call this motion adjournment of debate or postponement of debate.

Take from the Table (Resumption of Debate)

A tabled topic may be taken up for discussion again by a motion, which is permitted only after another topic has been closed or tabled. The motion is usually debatable and typically requires a simple majority to pass. If the motion is successful, the tabled topic becomes the current topic, and all working papers, resolutions, and amendments attached to it are once again on the floor. Speeches restart according to the tabled speakers' list.

Closure of Debate

A successful motion to close debate means the end of debate on a substantive matter and immediate voting by the body on the matter. The motion is sometimes called "motion to move the previous question." The requirements for the motion are stringent: Almost all conferences allow debate on the motion (some only allow speeches against closure) and require a two-thirds majority to pass it.

Voting Procedure

Voting procedure consists of voting by the body on substantive motions that are alive on the floor. Voting procedure immediately follows a successful motion for closure of debate. Once in voting procedure, chamber rooms are secured, which means a staff member will stand by the door and physically resist attempts of anyone outside to open the door, and no one can enter the room or leave it. Some conferences also ask nonvoting delegates, observers, and chaperons to leave the room. Only motions related to voting and parliamentary points, except motions for adjournment, recess, and caucus, are in order during voting procedure.

Ordinarily, each delegation has one vote with equal weight, and a substantive motion requires a simple majority to pass. However, there are some exceptions. In Security Council simulations, a negative vote by any permanent member (China, France, Russia, the United Kingdom, or the United States) constitutes a veto and the automatic failure of the motion, regardless of the tally of other votes. Many conferences have Experimental Security Councils, which may have additional permanent members with veto power. Some conferences will also have nonconventional bodies in which weighted voting (e.g., an IMF simulation) or different veto powers (e.g., a national cabinet simulation) may be in effect.

The way voting works is simple: The chair will ask all those in favor of a substantive motion to raise their placards; then, all those against it to do the same; and finally, all those abstaining. The chair counts all votes, makes sure the three numbers add up to the total of those present and eligible to vote, and then announces the outcome.

Some conferences will vote on all substantive motions at the end of debate, in the order they were proposed, with amendments voted on before their related resolutions. Other conferences deal with amendments as they come along. Whatever the method, the voting procedure itself remains the same. As far as the order among resolutions and amendments is concerned, the standard practice is to vote on the proposals in the order they were submitted, although some conference rules allow the body to change this order. Some conferences also vote on amendments in descending order of complexity; that is, among the amendments to a particular clause, the one altering that clause in the most substantive way is voted upon first, then the one with the second most substantive changes, and so on. The order is set by the dais and is oftentimes very challenging to determine.

Adoption by Consensus

Some conference rules allow motions for adoption of a substantive motion by consensus or by acclamation, as some conferences call it. If there is such a motion, the chair asks the members of the committee if there are any objections. If there is no objection, the proposal is automatically adopted. A single objection is enough to defeat the motion and require voting on the proposal through regular voting procedure.

Abstentions

Few delegate guides clarify the issue of abstentions, and even fewer chairs are confident about how to handle them. The standard rule is that abstentions do not count against the majority. This simply means that abstentions are ignored (not counted as a vote) and that majority is calculated on the basis of "yes" and "no" votes only. To give an example, in a body with one-hundred delegates, simple majority means fifty-one votes. If, however, there are twenty abstentions, simple majority is then forty-one votes.

However, in the Security Council, abstentions work in a different way. Regardless of the number of abstentions, nine affirmative votes are required for passage of motions. In Experimental Security Councils, this number may be different.

Abstentions are in order only on substantive matters and can only be used by those delegations that identify themselves as "present" (and not "present and voting") during roll call.

There is another point of view that holds that whatever the ratio may be, a "yes" vote by 50 percent plus one of all those present and eligible to vote is required, regardless of what the "non-yes" votes are—they can all be abstentions, all "no" votes, or anywhere in between. This point of view argues that a majority (or any percentage) requirement means that the number of members entitled to vote corresponding to that majority must be in favor of the proposal. If you exclude abstentions, you can pass a substantive motion even with a single vote. For example, in a committee of twenty-five members, if twenty four are unsure and would prefer to abstain and the twenty-fifth delegate is in favor of the motion and if everyone votes according to these preferences, then the motion passes, with 100 percent support. This approach does not regard abstentions as votes, whereas in reality, there is only 4 percent support for the motion—not much legitimacy for a "successful" substantive motion. Admittedly, such a situation happens rarely, if ever, in practice.

Division of the Question

Dividing the question means separating a proposal, in this case meaning a draft resolution, into parts and then voting on each part separately. A motion to divide the question is in order once the committee is in voting procedure, but voting has not begun.

Most chairs and delegates dread dividing the question for two reasons: first, it is a lengthy procedure; second, and I think more of a factor in their dreading it, they do not understand it. However, division of the question, as lengthy as it may be, is pretty straightforward. Here is a shortcut, followed by an explanation of the entire procedure:

- Motion to divide fails → standard voting.
- Motion to divide passes → (1) collect proposals for division methods from delegates; (2) put the methods in order from most to least complicated (from most number of divisions to fewest divisions) and then order the methods with identical degrees of complication according to the order in which

they were proposed; (3) vote on the methods according to this order; (4) vote on the substantive question using the first method adopted, and if no method is accepted, vote on the whole proposal; (5) all adopted parts become part of the proposal; the rest do not; (6) if the rules require a final approval as a whole of all the approved parts, vote on all these parts as a whole.

Some conferences will allow only resolutions to be divided and not amendments. The reasoning behind dividing the question is that there may be enough support for certain parts of a proposal but not for it in its entirety, and by dividing the question, at least some parts of the proposal may be successfully adopted. This system does usually increase the possibility at least part of a proposal will be adopted, because delegates' preferences vary and voting on a proposal as a whole sometimes tends to create negative votes due to opposition to only a small portion of the proposal. Sometimes, though, the opposite is true, and delegates choose to vote against parts of a proposal because another part has been rejected and they feel the two parts should be either both adopted or both rejected. However, this is rare, and dividing the question usually helps to increase the proposal's chances of adoption. If there are any objections to a motion to divide, and there almost always are, the motion is usually debatable and typically requires a simple majority to pass. Some conferences allow the motion to pass only if all sponsors of an unamended resolution are in favor of the motion.

At most conferences, if a motion to divide the question is successful, the body has only *decided to divide* the question. The next procedural step is to accept proposals on the method to divide.[2] The chair will call on delegates to offer proposals, and most chairs will grant priority

---

2   Some conferences do not split these two steps into two separate motions. Once a motion to divide the question has been passed, these conferences will automatically pull out each operative clause of a proposal for separate voting on each clause, which is essentially what is done when voting clause by clause, as explained below, although the two are technically different procedures. While this process may take a long time, especially for lengthy resolutions, it may still be shorter than debate on various methods of division.

to the delegate who proposed the division. Preambulatory clauses of a resolution cannot be divided. Dividing the question means dividing between clauses, not dividing out clauses. In other words, if you would like to separate clause five from the rest of the resolution, the correct method is to divide between clauses four and five, as well as between clauses five and six, thus creating three parts. Some rules will allow division between subclauses; others will not. Under no circumstances, though, can a single-part clause or a subclause be divided. After all proposals have been made, they are ordered from most to least complicated—meaning, from the most number of divisions to the fewest. Those proposals of equal degree of complexity are ordered in the sequence in which they were proposed.

Once the ordering is complete, the body begins voting on the proposed methods as they have been ordered. The requirement for adoption of a method of division is generally simple majority, and the first method to be adopted is the method used in voting. If all proposed methods fail, then the proposal is voted on as a whole. If and when a method has been adopted, each divided part is voted upon according to the general rules governing voting procedure. All those parts that are adopted make up the final proposal. If no parts are adopted, then the proposal as a whole automatically fails, and customarily no additional voting on it as a whole is permitted. The final proposal, as made up of all and at least one approved part, is then voted upon as a whole (some conferences may not require this final step).

Voting Clause by Clause

A variation of dividing the question is to vote clause by clause on a resolution. This means that the committee will vote on each operative clause of a draft resolution separately and then vote as a whole on the adopted clauses. Many conferences do not require a debate or vote on a motion to vote on a resolution clause by clause, while some require a majority or lower vote to pass the motion.

Important Question

Although it is rarely used, making a resolution an important question means, in practical terms, raising the threshold for its adoption, usually from a simple majority to a two-thirds majority, as in the real UN rules. The motion is customarily in order only immediately before the vote on a resolution, before or after voting on amendments and division of the question, depending on the rules of the specific conference. If granted, the motion is generally debatable and will typically require a simple majority to pass, again the same as in the real UN. Some topics may be preset as important questions or some committees, such as the Security Council, may already be working on an important question principle at all times.

As in the real UN, the motion is usually applicable only in the GA and only under limited circumstances: recommendations with respect to the maintenance of international peace and security, the election of the nonpermanent members of the Security Council, the election of the members of the Economic and Social Council, the election of members of the Trusteeship Council, the admission of new members to the United Nations, the suspension of the rights and privileges of membership, the expulsion of members, questions relating to the operation of the trusteeship system, and budgetary questions. Some rules may allow new important question categories to be established. It is important to remember that the Security Council has priority over the GA or any other body on issues regarding the maintenance of international peace and security.

Roll Call Vote

A motion for a roll call vote will customarily have a low majority or a plurality requirement. Many conferences accept the motion automatically. A successful motion means the vote on the substantive motion (roll calls are out of order on procedural matters) will be taken in alphabetical order, either starting with the first delegation in alphabetical order or with the delegation whose name is chosen by a draw, with standard vote options (yes, no, abstain) still available as well an additional option of pass. Members who pass will be asked for their votes again after roll call has been completed and will typically be required to vote yes or no and not allowed to abstain. Passing twice is not permitted, either, and if abstentions are in order, attempting a second pass will mean an abstention. Roll call voting is generally automatic in Security Council simulations.

Change of Vote

If permitted in the rules, after a roll call vote and before the outcome is announced, the chair will ask if any member wishes to change his or her vote. At this time, with no need for an explanation, delegates may change their vote. Double changes are not allowed.

Right of Explanation of Vote

Many conferences allow members to explain their votes before or, more typically, after the body has voted on a substantive matter, but usually before the outcome is announced. Right of explanation is ordinarily in order only if a roll call vote is taken, but some conferences grant the right in ordinary voting as well. The time allocated to a right of explanation is usually short—most often under a minute. Although some conferences will allow any member to explain his or her vote, with a maximum number of such speeches permitted, this right is typically granted only to those who have voted in a way that appears to be contrary to their stated position on the substantive motion during debate. While this is obvious in some cases, it can and does become tricky for a chair to determine, because many delegates never explicitly state their positions during debate and their speeches can even be interpreted as supporting both sides. Some conferences do not permit sponsors of a proposal to explain their votes.

Reconsideration

After a substantive motion has been voted on, a motion to reconsider—that is, to vote on the motion again—is in order. Ordinarily, such a motion can be made only by a delegate who voted on the prevailing side, is generally debatable, and typically requires a simple majority or two-thirds majority to pass. If the motion passes, the proposal is deemed not to have been voted upon at all. In some conferences, it is in order to move to reconsider after at least one proposal, but not necessarily all proposals, has been voted upon. In others, the motion is in order only after the whole voting procedure on all substantive motions is over. If the latter method is used, a successful motion to reconsider a resolution will typically be required before a motion to reconsider an amendment to that resolution can be made.

Resolutions

In order for a resolution to get on the floor to be discussed, a certain fraction of the body's membership must express a desire for its introduction. Such a desire can be expressed by delegates in two ways: by being a sponsor to the resolution, usually reserved exclusively for the authors of the resolution; or by being a signatory, expressing no position on the content of the resolution but nevertheless stating that the resolution warrants consideration.

The number of sponsors and signatories required for a resolution varies from conference to conference and from committee to committee, but 10 percent to 30 percent of the whole body is typical; that includes sponsors plus signatories. Many conferences make no distinction between sponsors and signatories and may delete all the names before distributing to the whole body the final and official copy of a proposed resolution. When the necessary number of delegations has put their names on a resolution, the dais (or a separate panel at some conferences) reviews it. They check the document for logical consistency, relevancy, grammar, spelling, punctuation, and format. They can make changes, ask for clarifications from the authors, and at the end of the review, approve or reject it, stating their reasons in the case of rejections. An approval does not mean support for the resolution; it simply means that it is in order and worth discussing.

An approved and distributed draft resolution becomes part of debate only after it has been formally introduced to the floor. This is done in one of two ways: as part of formal debate, when a sponsor's turn is up or he or she has been yielded to; or by suspending formal debate for the purpose of moving the draft resolution onto the floor. In either case, the sponsors read aloud the resolution and answer nonsubstantive questions about it with no time limit on either activity. In rare instances, a member of the dais performs these duties. Preambles are not supposed to be read aloud as they are permanent and nondebatable parts of a resolution. Nevertheless, most conferences will let them be read anyway. It is out of order to make any substantive reference to a resolution that has not yet been introduced to the floor.

Resolutions are very important; in fact, they are the only concrete final product of all the debate in a committee. I will come back to them in Chapter Six.

Amendments

In the course of debate on a resolution, the body as a whole, or some delegates, may feel the need to change it. The way to go about this is by submitting amendments. Amendments are generally short and come in a variety of forms: they add and strike words, sentences, or entire clauses, and change punctuation or words, all in an effort to make the resolution a better one. Many times, amendments arise out of compromises to provide more support for the resolution as a whole. Like resolutions, amendments need sponsors and signatories, but the minimum number required is generally much lower (10 percent is typical). Again, just like resolutions, amendments need to be approved by the dais before being moved onto the floor for discussion. Luckily, amendments usually move faster through the ranks of the dais, are subject to less strict review, are typically introduced by a staff member shortly after being approved, and do not need to be distributed to delegates. It is out of order to make any substantive reference to an amendment that is not yet on the floor. It is also not permitted to submit an amendment to an amendment being discussed.

Many conference rules prohibit the passage of contradictory amendments, a rule that for three reasons I have never quite understood. First, it is difficult to establish that two amendments are contradictory, as there are usually no guidelines. For example, is a budgetary appropriation of ten million dollars in contradiction to one of twenty million dollars? The two are different but not necessarily contradictory. However, many chairs would rule out of order an amendment of twenty million if one of ten million has already passed. Second, on a more theoretical point, if an amendment has been approved by the body, it is no longer an amendment but now a part of the draft resolution, no less so than any other part of the resolution that was originally there. So, an additional amendment intrinsically cannot be contradictory. Third, preferences change, and if the body feels the need to make multiple changes to a single sentence, the delegates should be given the option and opportunity to do so.

Friendly vs. Unfriendly Amendments

Many conferences make a distinction between amendments with unilateral support from the sponsors of the resolution and those without such support, calling them friendly and unfriendly amendments, respectively. If such a system is used, the chair, after dais approval, will ask the sponsors of the resolution if they consent to the change, and if each sponsor does so, then the amendment is automatically accepted and becomes part of the draft resolution. If even a single sponsor is in disagreement with the amendment, then it becomes unfriendly and is open for debate. On the other hand, many conferences make no distinction between amendments and consider all to be unfriendly and subject to debate and approval by the entire body. Conferences that do so are generally the same conferences that do not allow sponsor or signatory names to appear on distributed draft resolutions. The reasoning is that, once a proposed resolution has been approved for debate by the dais, it becomes the property of the entire body and, as such, any changes to it thereafter must be made by the entire body.

Working Papers

Similar in idea to a resolution, but not necessarily the same in format, a working paper is what the name suggests: ideas on paper and a work in progress. Working papers need dais review before being introduced, but this is usually a formality in order to make certain the document pertains to the topic at hand. Copies of working papers are often distributed untyped or with little formatting and with no formal introduction. Once on the floor, working papers provide a guideline for prospective resolutions. A working paper can be in perfect resolution format or just a list of ideas, points, or a paragraph—pretty much anything is acceptable to allow for a more flexible and efficient debate. It is out of order to make any substantive reference to a working paper that is not yet on the floor.

Recess (Suspension of the Meeting)

Recess is the suspension of proceedings at the end of a session until the following one, as scheduled. It is in order only at the scheduled end of a session, that is, before a meal break or at the end of the day's proceedings. It also requires that the body not be in voting procedure. Typically, this motion is not debatable and requires a simple majority to pass.

Adjournment (of the Meeting)

Not to be confused with adjournment of debate, adjournment is the closing of all proceedings for the conference. It is in order only at the scheduled end of the conference and requires that the body not be in voting procedure. Typically, this motion is not debatable and requires a simple majority to pass.

Point of Personal Privilege

A point of personal privilege may be made by a delegate if there is physical disturbance in the chamber, such as too cold a temperature or lack of decorum, which impairs his or her ability to participate in the proceedings. Points of personal privilege may not interrupt a speech unless the disturbance (such as a nonworking microphone) prevents the delegate from following it properly.

Permission to Approach the Chair

During formal debate or moderated caucus, some conferences allow requests by delegates to go up to the dais for the purpose of asking a question regarding a substantive motion or to discuss a personal matter if it pertains to the proceedings.

Point of (Parliamentary) Inquiry

A point of inquiry or parliamentary inquiry is a question about the rules of procedure. Such a point can be made by a delegate at any time except during a speech. The chair answers the question according to the rules of procedure. If a clear answer to a point of parliamentary inquiry can readily be found in the delegate handbook, then it should not be asked—it is expected that points of inquiry be made only on missing or unclear information in the rules.

Point of Order

A point of order can be made at any time except during the execution of another point of order and refers to the use of an improper parliamentary procedure by the chair. Inactivity by the chair in case of a procedural violation by a delegate is grounds for a point of order, too. If a speech, behavior, point, or motion is out of order, the chair is expected to call the delegate to order. For example, if a delegate is speaking without having being recognized and the chair does not stop the speech, both the delegate and the chair are out of order.

When a point of order is made, the chair weighs the point according to the rules of procedure and rules on it immediately; no discussion is allowed on the motion. When one point of order is under consideration, another one is automatically out of order. The chair has full discretion in recognizing points of order, and most chairs do not appreciate points of order that interrupt a speech, unless it is absolutely necessary.

Appeal to the Decision of the Chair

A delegate may appeal any ruling or decision of the chair, except those that are designated in the rules as unappealable. For example, the granting of a motion for a right of reply or a motion to adjourn are typical unappealables. Normally, the delegate appealing a decision of the chair is allowed to speak for his or her appeal and the chair to speak in his or her defense. This procedure is used rarely and usually requires a high majority, such as two-thirds. If it passes, the decision of the chair is overturned at once.

Competence

In most conferences the competence of a body to address a topic, resolution, or amendment may be questioned by a motion. The motion is usually debatable and typically requires a significant majority, such as two-thirds, to pass. Ordinarily, conference rules will not allow topics on the provisional agenda to be challenged since they are preapproved by the Secretary-General. The motion generally has to be made before the body begins to discuss the matter, but in rare circumstances, conferences may allow it at any time before the closure of debate on the topic. When a motion challenges a proposed addition to the agenda, rules will again generally require that the motion be made before the vote to add to the agenda and that the body vote on competence before it votes on adding the topic to the agenda. This procedure, likewise, is executed slightly differently in some conferences, allowing even added topics to be challenged later on. When a motion challenging the competence of a body to discuss a topic passes, the addition of the topic (or the topic itself, if it is already on the agenda) automatically fails. As far as resolutions and amendments are concerned, a successful competence motion automatically means failure for the proposal. Normally, such a motion is made immediately before the proposal is put to a vote, but the rules of some conferences allow for a challenge at any time during debate on the proposal.

Referring a Resolution or Question

Some conferences allow committees to refer a resolution or a topic to another committee at the conference. The motion to refer will normally be debatable and require at least a majority vote to pass.

Making Motions

Any motion typically needs to be seconded before it can be entertained; points do not need seconds to be entertained. The following are some typical forms that can be used to make motions or points:

- "I move that ..."
- "Peru makes a motion that ..."
- "I make a motion for ..."
- "Motion to ..."
- "Point of ..."
- - "At this time a motion for ... will be in order. Is there such a motion?"

- "So moved."
- • - "Delegate, to what point do you rise?"
  - "I rise to a point of…"

The chairing staff can refuse to entertain motions that they deem dilatory. They can do so if they believe the motion would be disruptive for the proceedings, or if a similar one has been recently voted upon and rejected. The ruling is typically not appealable. When a procedural motion is entertained, a simple majority is usually enough for its passage. In case of a tie, some conferences consider the motion as having failed, while others allow a second vote on it.

Withdrawal of Motions

It is generally acceptable to withdraw a motion at any time before it is voted upon. Only the original proposer of the motion is allowed to withdraw it. It is perfectly in order for the same motion to be remade immediately after its withdrawal even though there is disagreement on whether the withdrawer may do so. Most rules do not explicitly state that a delegate may not make a motion immediately after withdrawing an identical one. Nevertheless, chairs will normally not allow this to happen. I believe this to be a fair judgment—if you want to see a certain motion on the floor, don't withdraw it only to make it again immediately.

Precedence

If motion A precedes motion B in the rules of procedure, whenever there is an attempt to make both A and B simultaneously (provided they are both in order), then A, if entertained, is always executed before B is. This is so even if the two motions are mutually exclusive, that is, even if the execution of A rules out the possibility that B can also be executed. Not surprisingly, the order of precedence of points and motions varies from conference to conference. One commonality among conferences is that statements from the Secretariat have precedence over all else. The following precedence lists are fairly conventional.

Parliamentary Points and Motions Always in Order (unless otherwise noted)

1. Point of Order
2. Appeal to the Decision of the Chair
3. Point of Personal Privilege
4. Point of (Parliamentary) Inquiry
5. Point of Information
6. Right of Reply
7. Motion to Adjourn the Meeting (out of order during voting procedure)
8. Motion for Recess (out of order during voting procedure)
9. Motion for Caucus (out of order during voting procedure)

Motions in Order Only During Formal Debate

1. Motion for Moderated Caucus
2. Motion to Close Speakers' List
3. Motion to Reopen Speakers' List
4. Motion to Lay on the Table (Motion to Adjourn/Postpone Debate)
5. Motion to Close Debate (Motion to Move the Previous Question)

Motions Valid Only in Voting Procedure

1. Motion to Challenge Competence to Adopt a Resolution or Amendment
2. Motion to Divide the Question / Motion to Vote Clause by Clause
3. Motion for a Roll Call Vote
4. Motion to Vote on Unfriendly Amendments
5. Motion to Make a Resolution an Important Question
6. Motion to Vote on Resolutions

Motions Valid Only After a Topic Has Been Closed or Tabled

1. Motion to Challenge the Competence of the Body
2. Motion to Add to the Agenda

3. Motion to Change the Agenda
4. Motion to Reconsider a Resolution or Amendment
5. Motion to Take from the Table (Motion to Resume Debate)
6. Motion to Open the Speakers' List (on the next topic)

Chapter Four:
The Conference

I. Conferences

Choosing a Conference

Conferences come in all sizes and shapes. Some have fewer than a hundred participants, while the biggest ones have several thousand delegates. As far as the format is concerned, most conferences have a mixture of large, medium-size, and small committees embracing simulations of various types of international organizations. Exceptions do exist—for example, some conferences have only small committees, most of which are Security Council simulations with a few others such as NATO flavoring the conference. There has also been a recent rise in the number of conferences that only have multiple simulations of a single international organization such as the African Union or the Arab League.

I have attended all types of conferences, and I like small and medium-size conferences (with around six hundred delegates) much more than large ones. The reason is simple: in general, the smaller the conference is, the more personal it is, the better the quality of debate is, and the more competent the chairing staff is. I detest being stuck in a GA committee of a huge conference with two hundred other people and having to wait for hours for my turn to come up on the speakers' list. Smaller conferences give you more opportunity to interact with other delegates and staff members, even from other committees. Even if you are in a GA committee of a small conference, you will have the chance to work with everyone in the committee. Nevertheless, many schools must prefer large conferences, as evidenced by the fact they do indeed exist. Larger conferences are usually more aggressive with their marketing, more flexible with delegation sizes and changes to that size, offer a larger array of simulations, and are generally in larger cities, making travel and accommodation easier. And some delegates actually prefer large committees.

In addition to size, there are a few other factors to consider when choosing a conference. First, the timing of the conference is important. It should fit in well with other activities, such as exam and vacation times, and it should give ample time for preparation. It is also a good idea not to attend two conferences within a short period of time. Second, ease of travel and cost are important factors. Attending a Model UN conference can be expensive, especially if it requires flying. Registration fees and other costs vary too; some conferences are much more expensive than others, and accommodation and food in big cities are usually costlier than in smaller places. Finally, the quality of the conference, or in other words, your expected return from the conference, is very important. The quality of a conference is judged by your past experiences with it, the reputation of the conference, the quality of committees and topics, and location. Location means two things: which city the conference is held in and where in that city it is held. What I mean by the latter is whether the conference is held in a hotel, conference center, or on campus. I like on-campus conferences much better but there are a few left these days. A great source for finding a suitable conference for your team is the "Model UN Calendar" available on the UNA-USA website, which lists hundreds of conferences from all around the world, categorized by region, with basic information about each conference such as size, dates, committees, and fees as well as contact information.

When picking a conference, it is a good idea to do a lot of research and ask a lot of questions. Two seemingly similar conferences may offer two very different experiences. Organizing a conference is a huge undertaking and some conference organizers are much better than others at taking their job seriously, choosing the right topics, providing good service before and during the conference, integrating technology into the committees, and picking the right staff members for their committees.

Financing

Conference fees vary greatly. Delegation fees can be as low as $25 (or its equivalent in local currency) and as high as $150 or more, and delegate and faculty advisor fees vary within the same range too. Accommodation also varies, depending on the city, the type of hotel, and how many people share a room. Through special arrangements, hotels will usually accommodate up to four people in what is usually a double room. Even so, the nightly per delegate cost may be higher than $50, but typically will be half that. Some schools (especially those that have their own conferences) sponsor or subsidize these fees, but most students usually have to pay them out of their own pockets. Of course, it is possible to find sponsors to help subsidize costs. Many corporate sponsors are willing to provide financial assistance for educational activities such as Model UN. It is also worth looking at the local level for financial support, such as educational NGOs or the local Rotary Club. Another option for Model UN clubs to raise money for their trips is to organize fundraising events such as bake sales. Some conferences also offer housing with students of the organizing school for free or a nominal fee. When this is an option, it is not only a great way to save money but also a wonderful opportunity to get to know your host and possibly a new culture, if the conference is in a foreign country.

Delegations

Most delegates at the conference will be representing a UN member country, but in larger conferences, you may have nonmember delegations. These may be nonmember nations, observer entities, intergovernmental organizations (IGOs), nongovernmental organizations (NGOs), UN specialized agencies, and the press. Currently, the first category includes only the Holy See. Examples of IGOs are the African Union, the Caribbean Community, the European Union, the League of Arab States, and the International Seabed Authority. Typical NGO observers are Amnesty International, Greenpeace, and the International Red Cross. You may have any UN agency as an observer, from the International Atomic and Energy Agency to the International Fund for Agricultural Development; from the International Labour Organization to the World Health Organization. These observer agencies should not be confused with the same organizations running as committees at the conference (see below).

Country Assignments

Conferences use a combination of two major factors in assigning countries to delegations. First is the order of registration—the earlier a school registers for a conference the more likely that the countries it requests will be available. The second factor is the reputation and track record of the delegation. Organizers are more likely to assign first choices to their long-term "customers." Organizers also have insights, for various reasons, into the strength of the delegation and are more prone to assigning more popular countries to those delegations they deem strong. The five permanent members and other regional powers are usually the most popular.

There are, of course, advantages to representing a country such as the United States, for example. It is easier to make your voice heard and easier to find resources on the country, as well as its views on issues. But at the same time, it makes the delegation's life that much more difficult. For one thing, expectations will be higher. Additionally, other delegates will be more likely to know about the country and its views, so preparation needs to be more thorough and precise. I have represented some small countries and some big ones, including permanent members, and each one had its advantages, disadvantages, and challenges. There are also personal factors such as the background of team members and their academic interests, which become important in picking a country.

Types of Delegations

Model UN groups differ in size, structure, and goals. Some are extracurricular Model UN clubs, some are debate teams also participating in Model UN, some are part of a class, and some are informal groups. Depending on the nature of the group and its members, a delegation's orientation and goals may differ. While some participants may be grade-oriented students, others may just be looking for a fun weekend.

The Head Delegate/Permanent Representative

For college teams, the head delegate is usually solely responsible for the delegation, carrying out all of the responsibilities of a faculty advisor (see below) as well as being a delegate. For high school teams, the head delegate is more of a figurehead who helps the faculty advisor or chaperone. Some conferences do not assign the head delegates to any committees and ask that they be floating delegates, providing liaison services with the Secretariat, sitting in committees to evaluate delegates, helping team members, acting as the official lobbyer, cutting deals, providing extra research, and so on.

The Faculty Advisor

The faculty advisor's main role is to work with and prepare delegations before the conference, in organization, logistics, and content. He or she will handle tasks such as choosing conferences, conference registration, communicating with conference organizers, assigning students to committees, and making travel arrangements. The faculty advisor will also guide students through their research and organize meetings and mock sessions for content and rules of procedure preparation.

Typical Committees

The rule of thumb is that if a committee exists in the UN System, then it is fair game for a Model UN conference to include it. For this reason, it is not possible to give a laundry list of committees; anything within the UN System is a possible choice for a committee in a conference. I have provided a list of popular non-UN and inventive simulations below, and that list is by no means all-inclusive nor does it indicate that all or any of these committees will be found at a conference. Nevertheless, most conferences will follow a certain pattern. The committees will be divided into the General Assembly, the Economic and Social Council, and Specialized Agencies. However, do not be surprised when you find WHO in the GA, or the Security Council as part of the Specialized Agencies, because this does not reflect the real structure of the UN System.

The GA/ECOSOC/Specialized Agencies format of a Model UN conference does not necessarily follow the real UN format and will typically be arranged to accommodate the size of the conference. The GA will have the largest committees; ECOSOC will have medium-size ones; and Specialized Agencies will contain the smallest committees. It is also important to note that the real membership of a body is not necessarily exactly replicated at Model UN conferences. Especially for GA committees, in which all UN members and many observers are represented, fewer members will be present than would exist in reality. Furthermore, members may be added or removed, and sizes of committees altered. The same is true of topics—they will not necessarily be the same as the ones discussed by the real organization. The most popular committees are as follows: GA Committees (GA's Fourth and Fifth committees are less popular than the others), Security Council, Experimental Security Council, Historical Security Council, HRC, ICJ, NATO, UNCTAD, UNDP, UNEP, WHO, WTO, and national cabinets.

One final remark is about the number of delegates in a delegation. While smaller committees usually have one delegate per nation, larger ones may have up to three delegates representing a single country.

Examples Non-UN and Inventive Committees

- African Union
- European Union
- Experimental European Union
- Experimental NATO
- Future Security Council
- Historical Security Council
- League of Arab States
- National cabinets (British, French, Israeli, Russian, and U.S. are common)
- NATO
- Organization for Security and Cooperation in Europe
- Organization of American States
- Peace talks/summits
- Press corps
- Provisional governments
- Simulation of a historical or inventive crisis

Press Corps (Press Delegation, International Press Delegation)

Some conferences include a press committee, the members of which do not represent a country but rather report the events at the conference and from each committee. Thus, it is not really a simulation, because in the real UN, individual reporters and agencies follow the work of the organization. In the Model UN setting, the press corps reports on the simulations and keeps the other delegates informed about the rest of the conference through a daily newsletter. In order to be a press corps delegate, interest is more important than anything else, but due to necessary use of technology to publish the newsletter and the limited time available at the conference for training, experience with writing, photography, journalism, reporting, and publishing software is a plus. Press corps members are also expected to be familiar with international affairs and the ways of Model UN.

Members of the press corps are either assigned to one committee or rotate or float (between caucuses and faculty advisor meetings, for example). One or more staff members will lead and supervise the group. The press corps usually spends more time working than other delegates, because they must gather material during other committees' sessions and put everything together to produce the newsletter after the sessions end. As a delegate or a delegation, it is a good idea to generate publicity by actively providing information to press corps delegates either informally or by holding a press conference or interview.

Staff

Generally, the organizers of a conference will be separate from the participants, but exceptions do occur in which participating schools also take part in planning before and chairing during the conference. The staff is headed by the Secretary-General, who delegates much of the work but still works at least as much as any other staff member and supervises the work of all other staff members. The staff does everything from chairing committees to providing security at the hotel, to making copies of resolutions, and to organizing delegate events. There are two main types staff: the Secretariat (including the administrative staff), which organizes all of the logistics of the conference and oversee the work of the committees, and the committee staff. They are all there to help you—if you have any problems or questions about anything, you should go to them. Most of these people are experienced MUNers and will be able to answer your questions or direct you to the right person. They are helpful and courteous and in return expect the same courtesy and cooperation from the participants.

II.   At the Conference: Scheduled Events

Schedule

Although there are longer and shorter conferences, a typical weekend conference runs from Thursday evening through Sunday afternoon. Your schedule may look like this:

Thursday	
Registration	noon to 7:00pm
Opening Ceremonies	7:00pm to 8:15pm
Committee Sessions	8:30pm to 11:30pm
Friday	
Colloquium	10:00am to noon
Committee Sessions	1:30pm to 5:30pm
Dinner Break	5:00pm to 7:00pm
Committee Sessions	7:00pm to 11:00pm
Saturday	
Committee Sessions	9:00am to noon
Lunch Break	noon to 1:30pm
Committee Sessions	1:30pm to 6:00pm
Delegate Dance	9:00pm to midnight
Sunday	
Committee Sessions	9:00am to noon
Closing Ceremonies	noon to 1:30pm

Longer conferences will typically have dedicated lobbying days or times, more panels, and other events, but regardless of the length of the conference, committee sessions will make up the bulk of the schedule.

Opening and Closing Ceremonies

These two can be either the most boring or the most entertaining parts of the whole conference. Opening ceremonies will usually begin with a welcome speech from the Secretary-General, followed by lots of administrative details from the Secretariat, sometimes a moment of silence, and end with a keynote speaker, usually an ambassador, a diplomat, or a professor: in short, someone whose résumé is impressive and thus invites attention. The keynote speech is usually followed by a question and answer session with the speaker. I have heard some amazing keynote addresses and some terrible ones. The weightiness of the speaker's résumé is not necessarily a good indicator of the quality of the speech you will hear. Nevertheless, if you are already there, you might as well pay attention and try to make the most out of it. And if you are lucky, the speaker will be an expert on the topics you will be discussing, or even the very person you will be role-playing. In either case, ask any questions you might have after his or her speech and then try to catch up with him or her after opening ceremonies for a quick chat. Some opening ceremonies may also include a form of entertainment like a short concert. These are usually fun and spice up the normally chaotic and stuffy environment. The most ceremonious moments at each event are when Secretary-General officially opens and closes the conference: "I hereby declare the Tenth Session of … open/closed."

Plenary Session/Meeting

While all of the work at a conference is done in the individual committees, some conferences gather a joint meeting of all committees (or only the GA committees) at the end of the conference, at which each resolution that was passed in individual committees is discussed again and voted upon one more time. The debate time is usually very limited on each resolution, and amendments are out of order. Every resolution normally makes it through again, because the delegates who initially voted for it are still there with the rest of their delegations and it is unlikely that anyone will change his or her vote.

Head Delegate Meetings

Held usually once a day during the conference, these meetings are excellent tools to relay to the Secretariat any problems or concerns that delegations may have, and they serve as a forum for discussing feedback. Organizers value these meetings because they use them to take care of any problems and improve the conference for future years on the basis of the suggestions they receive.

Faculty Events

Most conferences will hold faculty meetings, much like the head-delegate meetings mentioned above. There may also be faculty meals, or additional talks or colloquia, when delegates are in session, depending on the conference. Additionally, most conferences offer a faculty lounge for a quick coffee break and meeting and exchanging ideas with other advisors.

Talks, Colloquia, Lectures

When committees are not in session, many conferences (usually collegiate) offer talks, colloquia, or lectures by professors and experts on specific issues. These forums offer an excellent opportunity to meet prominent people and talk to them about current issues.

Concert

You may have a small concert by a school band or an a cappella choral group at the opening or closing ceremonies or a longer concert as part of the delegate dance.

Dance/Get-together

Almost every conference has a dance or some sort of get-together at some point during the conference. These events are usually a good opportunity to relax and to get to know your fellow delegates.

III.   At the Conference: Things to Do

Town Offerings

You will have little time left from the conference to do anything else in addition to Model UN, but try to explore the attractions and cultural offerings of the city. At weekend conferences, for example, Friday morning will generally be free. Depending on where you are, that will give you enough time to walk around town or visit a museum. Also, use the days on which sessions end early (typically Saturday and Sunday, if your travel arrangements allow for it) to explore your surroundings. At Yale, we always encouraged students to take campus tours and to visit the museums of the University. Many took our advice, and I believe they had a more fulfilling experience than the rest of the participants.

Team Dinner

It is a great idea to organize a team dinner on one of the nights during the conference, preferably Saturday night, because of the time flexibility on that night. It is a good way to relax, have some fun, and bond as a team. Ask your faculty advisor or team leader to arrange it.

Briefings

The only required event for many teams, apart from the sessions, is to attend the daily briefings at the end of the day's sessions. The whole team gathers in one of the hotel rooms, and everyone shares with the rest of the crew his or her experiences and observations from the day's proceedings. These sessions provide an opportunity to compare your committee experiences with those of everyone else. They are also an excellent tool to assist teammates who may need help with topics or who may be frustrated about certain things in their committee. It is also the only time during the day when the whole team is together and is great for creating a team spirit.

Rooming

People who room together at a conference often end up becoming good friends. I suggest you room with people you do not already know well and try to get to know them over the course of the conference. I have made some great friends in Model UN, and many of them were my roommates at a conference.

Committee People

There will be many people from all sorts of backgrounds in your committee, some of them from places you may have never heard of and will never see. I find this fascinating and have always tried to get to know and keep in touch with as many people as I could. A friend of mine was in the same committee with the same person from Venezuela at an American conference two years in a row and later ended up visiting him in Venezuela while he was traveling through South America. When you spend time with the people in your committee outside of session, try not to talk "business;" go out for lunch together, have a cup of coffee, and try to get to know them as individuals. I have met some amazing people from all around the world at conferences and still keep in touch with many of them.

IV.   Conduct

There are many rules, written and unwritten, that participants at a Model UN conference will be expected to follow. While you may not like some of them, they exist for a reason and have been instituted for your safety and enjoyment of the conference. Cooperating with staff members and complying with the rules are good ideas, as it will make everyone's life easier and the experience more fruitful and fun. The basic idea is to act like international diplomats and in accordance with international norms and standards, and to follow the principles of the United Nations Charter. One can get into serious trouble, or even be expelled, for not following the rules— this includes everything from dress code and courtesy to sexual harassment and drug use.

Dress Code

Model UN conferences are usually very particular about the appearance of their participants. Since this is a simulation of diplomacy, they want the simulators to look like diplomats. Western business attire or business dress is usually what is expected. This means a dress shirt, tie, jacket, and slacks for men, and an equivalent outfit for women. Unacceptable are T-shirts, jeans, shorts, sneakers, baseball caps, and such. Many conferences also forbid the wearing of national dresses, military uniforms, and armbands. If not dressed appropriately, you will probably not be admitted to the committee room or will not be recognized for debate. The Secretariat has the final say on all matters of appropriate attire, and it is a good idea not to argue with them.

Delegate Curfew

Middle and high school conferences generally have a curfew after which time delegates must be in their hotel rooms and quiet unless they are out with a faculty advisor. I do not know of any college conferences with a curfew, although they will enforce quiet hours at the designated conference hotels. In any case, there will be staff members patrolling the corridors to enforce the curfew or quiet hours.

Drugs and Alcohol

Illicit drugs are simply not tolerated at conferences. You should also follow the local laws and ordinances regarding alcohol. Failure to do so may result in expulsion from the event or even greater punishment.

CHAPTER FIVE:
THE COMMITTEE

I.   Logistics

The Room and Seating

There are two main setups for committee rooms: those in which you sit around a table and those in which you sit in chairs arranged in rows. If you are in a small committee, you will probably have the table setup, and the dais will be at the head of the table, usually close to the door. In a bigger committee room, you will see rows of chairs with an aisle running in the middle and the dais at the front, sometimes raised, facing the seats. If you are at an on-campus conference, your committee sessions may be held in a classroom or an auditorium.

There are advantages and disadvantages to each arrangement. Sitting around a table lets you see almost everyone at all times and gives you a tabletop to work on. On the downside, it is practically impossible to talk quietly to anyone about a resolution or anything else, as conversation is quite disruptive and very noticeable. The other disadvantage is that because you usually do not stand when giving a speech, it is harder to establish a sense of authority over the other delegates. In a row setting, on the other hand, it is easier to make quick exits with another delegate to discuss something or even to move around the room. It is also easier to multitask by following debate and working on an amendment at the same time, for example. On the downside, it is impossible to see everyone at once, unless you sit in the very last row, but then you only see everyone's back.

Whatever the setup, one thing is vital: always be on time. Chairs do not like delegates coming in late, and neither do other delegates.

Furthermore, a lot can happen within the first few minutes of a session, and you do not want to miss the action. Punctuality is relatively easy to accomplish. Perhaps more important and surely trickier is the matter of seating.

Where you sit throughout the conference will have a significant effect on your performance. It will be a factor in determining how well you observe and interact with other delegates and with members of the dais and how well you deliver your speeches. People usually stick with the seat they choose in the first session throughout the whole conference, so choose yours wisely, unless it is prearranged, which is usually the case in smaller committees.

Your choice of seating is very individual, so I will tell you what I used to do. In row seating, I always chose an aisle seat in one of the middle rows, for several reasons. First, an aisle seat gave me greater flexibility in getting up to deliver speeches, leaving my seat for whatever reason during proceedings, and stretching muscles (vital). Second, I found that such a centrally-located seat is the best one to observe other delegates and to interact with them. Third, it gave me the best chance of being recognized by the chair. Back seats are too far away and front seats are too close—chairs get self-conscious when recognizing delegates who are too nearby. Furthermore, when a chair looks up, he or she is more likely to perceive placards in the middle more easily.

The same logic applies when sitting around a table. The best seats are those that are on either side of the dais toward the opposite end of the table. Sitting directly across from the chair is not a very good idea, because chairs can become uncomfortable when making eye contact with and recognizing those delegates. Having said all this, sit where you will feel most comfortable, of course.

Chairing Staff (Dais)

The dais can be made up of anywhere from two to almost ten staff members who will have a strict hierarchical order among them.

Common titles for members of the dais are Chair, Vice/Deputy/Assistant-Chair, President, Vice/Deputy/Assistant-President, Director, Deputy/Assistant-Director, Moderator, Assistant Moderator, Rapporteur, Parliamentarian, Registrar, and Secretary.

Your delegate guide will clearly define each staff member's duties, and the hierarchy will be clear from the onset. Whatever it may be, there will always be a single boss, usually called the chair or director. The chairing staff is in charge of running the proceedings and maintaining order within the rights bestowed upon it by the Secretary-General. Even though the Secretary-General has full authority over all proceedings, he or she will normally not interfere directly in the proceedings, but he or she and designated Secretariat members still retain such rights as amending the rules, deciding on controversies, and dealing with order issues and emergencies.

The Secretary-General or a representative can interrupt proceedings to speak to the body—these will typically be administrative announcements, but they can pertain to any other matter. For example, at a conference I attended as a delegate, a school from a certain part of the world was distributing pictures and other propaganda material about an international dispute that their home country was involved in. After other delegates complained, Secretariat members went into every committee to collect the materials, apologize about the incident, and warn everyone that this was the wrong forum for such propaganda. They also talked to the head delegate of the team, who happened to be in my committee, and as he told me afterwards, threatened to expel his team at once if any more material was distributed during the conference.

II.   Debate

There are two components of succeeding at debate and attaining your delegation's goals. First is a comprehensive knowledge and use of the rules of procedure. Knowing when and how to use the rules will let you make the right point or motion at the right time. It will also help you gain precious floor time. Knowing how to yield, how to be yielded to, make comments, and rise to points of information is vital in getting your ideas across. Also important is the ability to tell when to opt for recognition. You will not be recognized every time you raise your placard, and if you are recognized for points that are not vital, you may be forgoing the chance of being recognized later on for a more important point. Second is the formal delivery of ideas, policy and negotiations. Ideas can sound great to you on paper, your country's policy may be so important as to affect an entire bloc's views on a topic, and resolutions may be amended and deals cut during caucus, but if you do not explain all of this to your peers in a logical, organized, and rule-compliant manner, you will not be able to sway opinions. You have very limited time to engage and persuade some very hostile, neutral, and disinterested delegates, and you must be able to use that time wisely. To these ends, a delegate must remain completely alert at all times.

Speeches

The ultimate purpose of a speech is to sway votes. By delivering to the rest of the body their ideas, delegates try to garner votes for or against a substantive motion. Thus, a good knowledge of the issues is vital in making speeches, but it is not enough. While knowledgeable delegates stand out initially and are listened to, it is those delegates who can deliver that knowledge in a logical and engaging manner with the right body language, the right tone of voice (loud and clear but not shouting), and the right timing who are the most successful delegates. Dry knowledge of facts is also not enough because delegates have to react to other speeches, make connections between arguments and facts, and answer questions. These communicative, theatrical, strategic, and analytical skills are just as important as having a good grasp of the facts of the matter.

While at the real UN almost all speeches are written by an army of advisors with unlimited resources, the typical Model UN speech is impromptu and delivered in reaction to the current debate. Unless it is an opening speech, it is hard to use in debate something you wrote before the conference. The simple truth is that you have to think on your feet.

I never wrote a speech during my Model UN career as a delegate, but before the conference I used to make notes of major points I wanted to get across in debate and then I used these in speeches during debate, usually early on since they would be general policy points. When it came to making speeches on resolutions or wherever the debate was leading to, I took notes on important points other delegates made, and also made notes on new points I wanted to make.

When delivering a speech, I would take my notepad with me with the points I wanted to make in short note form. Even so, I would try to remember these points because I do not like reading from paper but appreciate the comfort and security of having my notes with me in case I need them.

That being said, many delegates like to write out exactly what they want to say and do not seem to be able to speak in any other way. If you do choose to write speeches though, I suggest you not read them verbatim, as spontaneous-sounding speeches are usually more effective than written ones. Try to remember your speech and refer to your notes only occasionally and do not be afraid to substitute words.

When writing or taking notes to deliver a speech, you not only need to get your ideas across but you also need to find strong points in the speeches of your allies to support them and weaknesses in the speeches of your opponents to counter them. You also need to identify well which point you are making by using sentences like, "My nation believes that ...," or "We agree/disagree with the esteemed delegate from ... because ...."

Your speech needs to be well structured and should contain the right elements: statistics when debate calls for it, a little emotion or anger when necessary, as well as anecdotes or examples when you want to make a point stick in people's heads. The tone of voice (angry, happy, etc.) and the language (firm, conciliatory, etc.) should be used in an intelligent way. You also need to stick to the issues and avoid being sidetracked. You have limited time to get your ideas across and you cannot afford to spend that precious time talking about nonissues. Further, you may be called to order if your remarks are not deemed relevant to the subject or are simply dilatory.

It is a good idea not only to deliver your nation's position but also to justify it by referring to precedents in past UN or other international actions, resolutions, and studies, as well as referring to moral issues and citing UN documents, voting records, and other sources.

On the technical side, there are several important points to keep in mind when delivering a speech. First of all, you cannot speak without first being recognized by the chair. Even if it is your turn, wait for the formal recognition by the chair. Second, it is out of order to make any substantive reference to a draft resolution that is not yet on the floor. You can, however, talk about ideas being tossed around for a resolution or say this or that idea would be a great addition to a potential resolution. But be careful: delegates love rising to points of order when someone uses the word "resolution" in a speech. Even if you are in order (for example, if you simply say a certain point would be good to include in a resolution without referring to a particular resolution), the interruption is unpleasant. Third, it is generally not good, and in fact sometimes considered inappropriate, to say "I" when making a substantive point (but it is generally okay to say "I" when making procedural points). Instead say, for example, "my nation," "the Czech Republic," or "we as the delegation from Nepal." Similarly, you need to use the third person even when speaking directly to another delegate or a staff member ("Does the speaker believe that … ?," not "Do you think … ?"). Finally, you should be polite, respectful, and avoid the use of slang.

Common Modes of Address

- "Honorable/Distinguished/Esteemed delegates …"
- "Ladies and gentlemen of the house …"
- "Mr./Ms./Madam Chair, President, etc. …"
- "I have a preceding motion to make."
- "Honduras moves for a ten-minute caucus for the purpose of …"
- "I rise to a point of parliamentary inquiry."
- "Burkina Faso urges members of the Council to vote in favor of this constructive amendment."
- "I wish to speak in favor of/against this motion/resolution/amendment because my nation …"
- "I yield the floor (to my colleague from Nigeria)."
- "I yield the remainder of my time (to points of information)."

The Opening Speech

There are two types of opening speeches: official (on behalf of the whole delegation), and unofficial (first speech in a committee). Official opening speeches are allowed at some conferences during opening ceremonies and are delivered by one or more representatives of each delegation. The speech may state the general overall policy of the delegation or talk about a specific issue. The unofficial opening speech is the first substantive speech delivered by a delegation in a committee. The speech is a general statement of the policy and views of the country concerning the topic at hand. This is where you set your tone for the rest of the proceedings. Make sure your opening speech is concise, precise, with a clear beginning and end, and delivered firmly.

Yielding to Another Delegate

You may want to yield to another delegate for a variety of reasons. If you are collaborating with someone on a working paper, resolution, or amendment, and you each have different areas of expertise, yielding to each other may make sense. You may also want to yield to a representative from a bloc other than your own if doing so is likely to get you more support on an issue. Sometimes you may be on the speakers' list but have nothing or very little to say; yielding can make sense in such a situation, too.

By far the most important reason I yielded to other delegates was to get yields in return. Especially during heated discussions on resolutions or crises, speakers' lists can be quite long. The way to get around this without leaving formal debate is to be yielded to, ask questions, and make comments. Of these options, being yielded to gives you the most flexibility and usually the most amount of time. Have a few buddies in the committee who will agree to yield to one another—there is very little that can be said in two minutes that cannot be stated in one minute and fifty seconds. If you yield to someone, he or she will generally return the favor, but in general you should try not to yield as much time as you get from being yielded to. Thus, do not hesitate to ask for yields even if you do not offer anything in return. Do it well before the speaker's turn is up in order to be the first one to ask. Often, delegates have little to say and like to yield to others. Yielding to other delegates and being yielded to gives the impression that you cooperate well with others and that they are interested in hearing what you have to say. The more you are yielded to, the more your name is heard, and that is certainly a good thing.

Yielding to Points of Information

You must have a purpose when you yield to points of information. Few things will look worse than yielding to points of information and not receiving any from other delegates. Even worse is not being able to provide a good answer to a legitimate question. You can ignore provocative or unintelligent questions, but it is imperative that you know, for example, exactly what that scientific term in operative clause two of your very own resolution on global warming means. If you have just put forward new ideas, talked about a fresh resolution, especially if you helped in authoring it, or have given a controversial speech, yielding to points of information can make sense. Yielding to points of information looks good as it gives you an air of confidence and enhances your credibility.

Asking Points of Information

A point of information is technically a question, but in practice, it does not have to be limited to that. It is out of order to make a comment or give a speech when recognized to make a point of information. It is also out of order to ask "dilatory," "irrelevant," or "derogatory" questions. However, this does not mean that you cannot somehow manage to do any of these things; smart delegates know how to use the rules to their advantage without breaking them. Here are a couple of examples:

(Straightforward) Point of information: "What does the delegate think about clause four in resolution 3.2?"
Instead, say: "Seeing how nuclear proliferation is a threat to world security and that most members of this house agree on the importance of nuclear nonproliferation, what, if anything, does the esteemed delegate have to say about clause four of resolution 3.2?"

(Straightforward) Point of information: "Does the delegate not believe that the resolution authored by his delegation is not a strong enough measure to solve the problem at hand?"

Instead, say (if valid!): "Does the honorable delegate not agree with me when I say that the resolution does absolutely nothing to solve the immediate problems at hand and that this fits his country's national policy perfectly as that country benefits financially from the continuing situation?"

Some of the commonly used forms of points of information are as follows:

- "Is the distinguished delegate aware (of the fact) that ... ?"
- "Does the speaker (not) realize that ... ?"
- "What would the esteemed delegate say if I were to point out/state that ... ?"

Friendly Points of Information

Questions need not always be inquisitive or hostile; there is such a thing as a friendly question. Such a question can be asked rhetorically to state support for the speech just delivered, to help an ally in clarifying an issue, or just to show general support for the delegate or a substantive motion. Here are a couple of examples:

Point of information: "Would the honorable delegate not agree with me if I said that in the light of the current crisis the first thing we must do is to issue a condemnation of the latest developments?"
Reply: "I absolutely agree; a quick condemnation followed by further action is the most appropriate course of action at this time."

Point of information: "Does the delegate believe that resolution 1.2 also lacks in providing funding or suggesting ways for its provision for the mentioned project?"
Reply: "Thank you so much for pointing that out. Yes, that is yet another deficiency in this well-intended yet incomplete and inefficient resolution."

There is a fine line between a smart and an annoying friendly question (or a reply for that matter) and you should be well aware of it. A friend of mine told me of a delegate with whom he was in the same committee at a conference. Whenever this delegate received a friendly point of information, he replied: "Yes, yes! You are so right that if you weren't so far away I would kiss you now!" Funny the first time, less so after the second, his little joke became the biggest annoyance for the rest of the committee after the third time. Don't be that delegate!

Answering Points of Information

Some points of information will really be asked out of curiosity, such as a clarification on a remark you have just made. These are usually easy to answer, thus do so in a concise and to the point manner. However, some questions are harder to answer. They may be nonsensical, hostile, or bordering on rude, and worst of all is a legitimate question to which you have no answer. In such instances, your acting skills come into play. Do not be frustrated if you get such a question, or at least do not look as if you are. Just do as most talented politicians do and say something that in no way answers the question but still makes sense. And remember, you do not have to answer the question at all if you do not wish to; you can simply ignore it and say "Next point of information," or "I choose not to answer that."

Yielding to the Dais

Yielding to the chair can leave two different impressions: that you are confident about your speech or that you are afraid to answer questions or allow comments. You want to create the former impression.

No Yields: Comments

Most delegates only unintentionally allow comments, that is, they forget to yield, and thus comments become valid. It is generally a good tactic to avoid comments if you are not sure what will follow, but many experienced delegates, especially in later sessions of a conference when they have a feel for the committee and the dais, will intentionally allow comments. One reason may be that they are genuinely interested in reactions to the speech they have just delivered. Another may be that if the speech is an all-friendly one, say a speech on a compromise resolution, there is very little, if any, danger of a hostile comment. If you decide to allow comments, make sure that your speech did not have very controversial or hostile comments, that it did not have major holes or assumptions, and that the chair is a good moderator and will allow those comments that support your speech as well as those against it. You do not want to take the risk of being bashed after a speech and unable to reply.

Making Comments

When making a comment, make certain it pertains to the previous speech. But this does not mean a comment is only a statement of agreement or disagreement. You can, after you refer to a portion or the entirety of a speech, elaborate on it as long as you stick to the main theme. By the same reasoning, do not make a comment just for the sake of it; make certain you have an important or interesting point to make. Remember, comments are short, and it is impossible to critique the entire speech in a comment. Just touch upon the key points during your comment.

Being Off Policy (Out of Character)

Being off policy means acting contrary to your nation's policies. This happens quite often at Model UN conferences because the participants are not career diplomats and much of the time they have not done enough research before the conference. Adequate preconference preparation will assure that delegates follow their countries' policies effectively.

Although thorough research will give you the tools necessary to make an educated guess on issues you have not prepared for, there may be instances where you simply lack enough information about your country's policy to even guess. When this happens, ask another member of your delegation for help. If you are unable to find anyone to help, you can just keep quiet on the issue. You are not required to mention every single issue in your speeches. Alternatively, you can contact your "home government" (the dais or the Secretariat) for help. Most conferences will not coach you on issues but may nevertheless give you useful tips and general information that will help you answer your questions. Some conferences also provide research facilities, and the Secretariat may have resources available for delegates' use.

If you think that another delegate is acting off policy, and that this is hindering debate in a major way, you may want to warn him or her. If you choose to do so, make sure you are absolutely certain and that the off policy delegate did not just make a remark that you may have misunderstood or misinterpreted. More importantly, do it in a nonconfrontational manner. Instead of saying "You're wrong," it is better to say "Are you sure about what you said? I remember reading something to the contrary." Good chairing staffs notice major policy mistakes and may warn delegates. I do not suggest talking to the dais or the Secretariat unless the policy mistake has major potential effects on the outcome of debate, such as an unwarranted veto.

Caucus

While it is true that speeches are what usually win awards, it is certain that it is in caucus that most things get accomplished. You must use caucuses effectively and to your advantage. Try to talk to as many delegations and groups as possible to exchange ideas. Try to act as a leader to bring groups together and lower tension if everyone starts yelling at each other. Always be productive during caucus, or at least look that way, because the chairing staff will circulate around the room and listen in on caucusing groups to see which delegates are actually working and which ones see the caucus as no more than a coffee break.

Crisis Situations

In addition to predetermined topics, your committee may have a crisis topic. The crisis will likely be unrelated to any of the agenda topics, and thus it will challenge delegates and demand a general awareness of world events. Crises may be entirely fictional or a development in an already existing world situation. Crises are fun and challenging because they move at a fast pace and require outside knowledge. A crisis topic will usually be introduced by a special news report or a report from the Secretariat. As the committee reacts to the events, more reports, special delegates, and even video footage may follow.

Some conferences have midnight crises, dragging delegates out of their beds in the middle of the night to solve an international crisis.

Special Delegates and Expert Witnesses

Speakers may be called into the committee room to brief the chamber on a certain issue as part of a crisis script, on the request of the delegates during debate, or by the chair's discretion. These people might play the role of an NGO worker, a victim of persecution, an expert on a technical matter, the ambassador of a nation that is party to the conflict, a representative of an unrepresented nation, and so on. This facet of the program not only gives valuable information to the delegates, but also livens the proceedings by visualizing what would otherwise be written information. Rarely is the special delegate or expert witness allowed to take part in formal debate, but a question and answer session is usually granted after the formal speech or testimony.

III.   How to Use the Rules

Quorum

There are usually only two instances when quorum does not exist. One is at the beginning of sessions, either early in the morning or after a meal break when some delegates have not made it to the committee yet, and the other is when many delegates are outside of the committee room working on resolutions. In the latter case it is easy to recuperate quorum, but in the former, the committee is at the mercy of delegates who like to sleep late or enjoy long meals, which is unfair to the people who actually make it on time to the committee room and have to wait for the others before debate can begin. For this reason, I never liked challenges to the quorum as a chair and never challenged quorum as a delegate. Unless a vote is coming up, I see no point in challenging quorum and thus possibly halting debate.

Roll Call

This is straightforward. Your name is called, and you simply say "present," "here," or something to that effect. Remember, if you say "present and voting" you cannot abstain on substantive motions during voting. If you miss roll call, which I suggest you do not, send a note to the dais as soon as you come in, apologizing for your tardiness without giving an excuse (because no one will care) and asking to be included on the official attendance list.

Agenda

Adoption of the Agenda

Since most committees go through all topics on their agenda, I regard the issue of deciding the order of discussion to be unimportant, and I very rarely spoke on the adoption of the agenda when I was a delegate. Nonetheless, there are topics that your nation may prefer not to discuss or topics in which your nation is a major player and you may want to set the agenda in a certain way for strategic purposes. In such cases, it is a good idea to try to sway the committee to pick the order of topics that will benefit your country. Many delegates also like to speak on setting the agenda because it helps them warm up to debate and relieve tension or nervousness. Whatever the case, do not be confrontational or hostile during these speeches—it simply does not make sense as it is not substantive debate.

Take from the Table

In order for a tabled topic to be taken from table, the current one must be tabled first—only then will a motion to take from the table be in order.

Caucus

The best times for caucuses are either when resolution and negotiation ideas are flying around during formal debate and delegates want to discuss these ideas informally or when debate is wearing down because the delegates are becoming tired. Chairs do not like to entertain too many caucuses. When a chair is not willing to allow a caucus, it is best not to insist.

Moderated Caucus

You should ask for a moderated caucus when many delegates are willing to speak but do not find the chance because of the length of the speakers' list. Moderated caucus is a great tool for quick discussion of newly introduced resolutions, amendments, and crises.

Speakers' List

I suggest keeping your name on the speakers' list at all times. Even if you think you will not need the time, you can always yield to someone else or simply take your name off the list before your turn. A good technique is to prepare a few handwritten notes to the dais ahead of time that request to be placed on the list. Keep the notes handy in your folder or your pocket. You can take one of the notes with you when you get up to speak and leave it with the dais after your remarks are over, which will assure that you get placed on the list as quickly as is allowed by the rules.

Right of Reply

During my Model UN career, I received only a handful of requests for a right of reply as a chair and granted almost all of them. I was lenient with rights of reply, but I never let one be made without a caveat about the merits and dangers of it, as well as a thinly veiled threat of action if an offensive reply was made. Delegates generally use rights of reply to respond to comments about the country they are representing, but in rare instances, they are used by delegates who take personal offense to a remark made. I have only witnessed this happen once—we were not actors in a fictional proceeding for those short few moments, but we were simply human beings with different backgrounds and beliefs and one of us had unintentionally offended another. Do not ask for a right of reply after every sarcastic comment, but be sure to ask for one if the remark is clearly out of line.

Voting Procedure

<u>Abstentions</u>

You may want to consider abstaining on a substantive motion if it is essentially okay but nevertheless not acceptable as is because parts of it are against your nation's policies or it is not complete or effective enough.

<u>Division of the Question</u>

If you think parts of a resolution, but not the whole proposal, warrant adoption, ask to divide the question and make a division proposal that suits your policy.

<u>Important Question</u>

If you are opposed to a resolution, you may attempt to block it by moving to make it an important question. By raising the threshold for the adoption of the resolution, you are hoping that it will not gain enough support to pass when voted upon. But there is a catch: the simple majority that is ordinarily required to pass the motion to designate the resolution as an important question is usually the same as that needed for adopting the resolution itself. Conventional wisdom says that people in favor of the resolution will not vote to raise the threshold required for its adoption. Thus, if there is majority support for the resolution, then the motion will likely fail and the resolution will probably pass. Conversely, if the motion has enough support to pass, these votes will probably be against the resolution, too. So without making it an important question, they can defeat it! The only exception to this that I can think of is if there are some delegates who are in favor of a resolution yet feel that the topic is important enough to warrant a higher majority. Then, these delegates may vote for the motion, but this scenario is a long shot.

Am I suggesting that the use of important question is ineffectual? As long as both the motion and passage of a resolution require simple majorities, or the motion requires at least the same majority as the passage of the resolution, the answer is probably yes. Such is an example of the absurdity that grows out of the rules of procedure from time to time.

Roll Call Vote

It is a good idea to ask for a roll call vote if it is difficult to note other delegates' votes and if you would like to do so for reference on their stance on the issue. A roll call vote will give you an idea of where those "quiet" delegates stand. You can also see if any delegates have changed their minds and ask them their reasons.

Right of Explanation of Vote

If for some reason (and make sure it is a sensible one) you decide to change your position during voting procedure, I highly recommend that you ask for a right of explanation, provided it is in order. Even if the reason is obvious, such as a divided out and failed clause that you deemed indispensable, it is still a good idea to say that for the record in order to be certain that everyone is aware of it. It will also make you look like a delegate who sticks to his or her policy. Do not use the time to criticize or disparage other delegates or the outcome of the vote; what is done is done. A simple expression of discontent will get your message across without gaining enemies. Also, if the rules do not allow it, do not even think about asking for a right of explanation for a vote that was consistent with your position throughout debate. You will be denied and even if you are granted the right, what new things do you have to say that you did not have a chance to articulate during hours of debate on the topic, anyway?

So You Want to Veto, Huh?

Dumbarton Oaks participants realized the immense power their countries would possess in the aftermath of World War II, and they did not want to waste the chance to use that power to their advantage. They reached a decision: the five Great Powers (China, France, the Soviet Union, the United Kingdom, and the United States) would be the permanent members of the Security Council.

Later, at the San Francisco Conference, which formally established the United Nations, the most controversial issue was the proposed veto power of the Great Powers in the Security Council. The veto power was approved with one exception: with Australia taking the lead, the conference approved Article Twenty-Seven, which stated that a member who is party to a dispute could not veto proposals for peaceful means of resolving the problem (Chapter VI of the UN Charter – Pacific Settlement of Disputes). However, the permanent members retained their veto power against proposals for action such as economic sanctions or military intervention (Chapter VII of the UN Charter – Action with Respect to Threats to the Peace, Breaches of the Peace, and Acts of Aggression). Thus, the "equal" house of the United Nations, namely the General Assembly, became overshadowed by the superior Security Council.

Interestingly enough, although the United States was the strongest proponent of the veto, it did not use this power until 1970 because it usually found sufficient support from the rest of the Council so that resolutions against its interests were usually not even put to vote. On the other hand, the Soviet Union was almost the only country using the veto during the same period, and it did so a total of 105 times. The Soviet Union was politically isolated on the Security Council, and often the only way it could block a resolution was to use the veto.[1] After 1970, however, the United States used the veto more frequently than any other permanent member, including the Soviet Union and the Russian Federation when the new nation assumed the Soviet Union's permanent member seat following the break-up of the USSR.[2] After the fall of the communist regimes in the USSR and Eastern Europe, the veto has only been used occasionally, and none was on a serious security issue. Although there has been a significant decline in the use of veto power, the threat of it remains.

Just short of a veto, abstaining or voting affirmatively with reservations on a resolution places pressure on the Security Council and undermines its authority. For example, China either abstained or voted in favor with reservations on thirty-eight out of ninety-seven

---

1   Bruce Russett, ed., *The Once and Future Security Council* (New York: St. Martin's Press, 1997), 158.

2   With a dramatic decline, the Soviet Union and the Russian Federation used it only a total of four times from 1989 through 2007.

resolutions about Iraq between the invasion of Kuwait and the end of 1994.

The dramatic fall in the use of the veto power was largely due to the collapse of communism and the end of the Cold War. During the Cold War years, the Council often found it very difficult to fulfill its duties. The enmity between the Americans and the Soviets frequently led to deadlocks in the Security Council. In the aftermath of the Cold War, the tension has cooled down between the two states, and the world has changed much.

However, the end of the Cold War era did not mean the end of problems nor the end of conflicts or tension around the world. The problem of human security threatens the world we live in. Individuals and their human rights are under the threat of many factors such as extreme nationalism, fundamentalism, ethnic and religious conflicts, narcotics, and terrorism.[3] These problems are usually harder to detect and deal with than problems such as nuclear disarmament, because they are smaller and often more regional. The new security threats nevertheless affect the whole world in an age of increased communication and global economy, and one could argue that more of the issues at hand today concern smaller nations than did the security matters of the Cold War era.

The most important issue is stability, which does not simply mean the absence of wars. Rather, stability means prosperous economic systems and legitimate political regimes. Domestic stability cannot be separated from regional or global security. It is frequently asserted that the Security Council's primary duty and aim in today's world is to provide stability to every country and region. It is also widely believed that the Security Council needs to reform itself to be able to handle these issues. The Security Council needs to be more efficient in many ways, and the veto power is a handicap in today's Security Council.

Having gone through two world wars, the Great Powers were justified in being scared when the UN was founded of reliving the horrors of those wars. Thus, the structure of the United Nations, and specifically the Security Council, can be interpreted as a preventative

---

3   Longin Pastusiak, "Strengthening the Security Council" (working paper, Gdańsk University, Gdańsk, Poland, 1995), 2.

measure or a defense mechanism. But the privilege of permanent membership has been abused by all of the five permanent members, be it to gain political strength over other states or to gain economic advantages.[4] Hours spent in the chamber discussing an issue and days of negotiations and phone conversations can result in no solution because of a single "no" vote. Conversely, once the five permanent members have consensus on an issue, they need only four more members to vote affirmatively, a number not hard to get since regional distributions always place countries with similar political orientations as the Big Five on the Security Council.

Thus, the claims of many countries that they have almost no say in most matters discussed by the Security Council are valid. Costa Rica, as concerned as it may be about world affairs, possesses almost no power when it comes to making a decision about whether to place economic sanctions on Iraq or not. Larger states are discontent with the Security Council as well but for a slightly different reason than smaller states: they want the same power that the five permanent members have. Each has its own reason for wanting change. Germany and Japan bear much of the costs of the UN, specifically of peace-keeping operations, and almost no action is possible without the consent of these two countries. Countries such as Egypt, Brazil, and India feel they are important powers in their regions and would like to take on leadership roles. Others like Pakistan are important contributors to peacekeeping operations and would like to have a say in making decisions about them.

The world has changed much since the founding of the United Nations. Almost all former colonies are now independent nations. An organization initiated by 51 members now embraces over 190 nations, small and large. What is more, the most powerful countries at the time

---

4   China is a prime example of how economic concerns affect voting on the Security Council. China has on various occasions succeeded in receiving loans from the World Bank after voting affirmatively or abstaining on important "Western-oriented" resolutions. An example of such a resolution is Resolution 678, which called for the use of "all necessary means" to remove Iraq from Kuwait. On the other hand, the U.S. sometimes uses its power in the World Bank and the IMF as leverage against others—rewarding correct votes on the Security Council and punishing not so correct votes by blocking loans and agreements.

of the founding of the UN, namely the five permanent members, are not the most powerful five anymore. The very countries against which the UN was founded, Germany and Japan, are now major contributors to the organization as previously mentioned. In a world free of Cold War tensions but full of other problems, change in the UN and the Security Council is a must. There have been numerous studies within and outside of the UN on Security Council reform, but to this day there is no consensus on the issue. Proposals range from eliminating the veto all together to giving veto power to more nations, from creating rotating permanent seats with or without veto power to limiting the use of the veto. Whatever the UN does in the future about the structure of the Security Council, one thing is clear: the use of the veto power is not appreciated in the world arena, and if you happen to represent a veto power on the Security Council, you should avoid using it.

Point of Personal Privilege

The only legitimate time when you can interrupt a speech with a point of personal privilege is if you cannot follow that speech for a reason beyond your control. Other than that, wait for a quiet time between two speeches and rise for the point. It is acceptable to make the following points of personal privilege, among others:

- "I can't hear the speaker/chair because there is too much commotion/the microphone is broken/etc."
- "The room is too cold/too hot."
- "There is no more water for the delegates."
- "There isn't enough light in the chamber."

While not an exhaustive list, the following are not acceptable:
- "I need to go to the bathroom." (Just go without making it common knowledge)
- "My neighbor is talking too much." (Tell him to be quiet)
- "I'm hungry; can we take a break?" (Your delegate guide tells you when it's time to break for lunch)
- "I don't like this topic; let's change it." (Move to table it)
- "What does Rule Twelve mean?" (Wrong procedure—make a point of parliamentary inquiry)

Permission to Approach the Chair

Use this request only if the next caucus seems hours away and you have a legitimately urgent matter that cannot be taken care of by trading notes with the dais. Do not even think about interrupting a speech to make this motion. Wait for the current speech to end, and do not hesitate to request permission, even if the rules do not explicitly allow for it. Motions not already contained in rules can still be made, and the chair has discretion to entertain them. Make your unconventional request sound legitimate and formal, and the chances are the chair will grant it to you. Do be aware of the fine line though, as variations do not always work: "permission to approach the chair" sounds legitimate whereas "permission to talk to the vice-chair outside" sounds a bit bizarre at best.

Point of Parliamentary Inquiry

Read the rules carefully and try to learn them well before you arrive at the conference. Make a cheat sheet of precedence and voting requirements, if one is not already provided in your delegate guide. Know all of the key rules cold; even if you do not remember everything else, this sheet and your delegate guide will always be there in case you need to check something. Even the most experienced chairs keep a copy of the rules and a cheat sheet handy. There are very few questions regarding the rules that your delegate guide cannot answer, so make absolutely sure your question is not already answered or is not answered clearly enough before you rise for a point of parliamentary inquiry.

Having said that, as a chair, I never minded explaining the rules even if it was my tenth time explaining the same one, and most chairs will do the same. If it helps the session move more smoothly and makes the delegates happy, no problem. There will always be inexperienced delegates, those who just do not care to read the rules, and those who insist on using the rules according to their own wishes. Then there are the usual suspects: I do not recall a conference in which I or whoever the chair was did not have to go through voting procedure—it is confusing and comes up only a few times over the course of the conference. Nonetheless, chairs like delegates who know their rules much more than those who ask every two minutes what a point of parliamentary inquiry is!

Point of Order

Whenever possible, it is better to rise to a point of parliamentary inquiry instead of a point of order, especially when the violation is made by the chair. But it is perfectly acceptable to rise to a point of order when the chair does not stop a delegate from speaking out of turn or from making points that are out of order.

Appeal to the Decision of the Chair

Do not do it. I admit that there are just plain bad chairs. But even the most experienced and knowledgeable chairs make mistakes and deliver decisions that delegates do not necessarily like or agree with. If you think a decision is unfair or out of order, use other means to try to reverse the decision. As I have mentioned, a point of parliamentary inquiry is usually sufficient. If that does not suffice, a point of order can be used. If neither works, then the chair is probably either not adept enough or, intentionally or unintentionally, missing something vital in the rules. In either case, appealing to his or her decision creates only one effect—it offends them.

Regardless of the outcome of the vote on the appeal, the chair becomes frustrated, loses respect for the delegate who made the motion and for everyone else who supported it, and a menacing air takes over the room. Reasonable chairs notice and admit their mistakes. If they do not, there is not much you can do unless the mistakes are just too many to bear, in which case you can notify the Secretariat. Otherwise, bear with the chair.

A vice-chair of mine was once appealed to because she denied a motion to caucus. I was out of the room at the time, discussing a draft resolution with a couple of delegates, only to be dragged back into the room by one of my rapporteurs. I knew exactly what had happened because it was getting late and there were constant requests for caucusing. My vice-chair was right in denying the motion because we had already spent a great deal of time that evening caucusing and it just made sense to stay in formal debate. As much as I disliked giving the impression that I was overriding her authority, I took over the gavel because the delegates were in uproar, and she was almost in tears. I told the committee that I stood by my vice-chair's decision, that there was no legitimate reason for yet another caucus, that her ruling was perfectly in order, that I would have ruled the same way, and finally that appealing to such a procedural matter was just not productive. The appeal failed by a landslide, but its effects lasted until the end of the session. Just do not do it!

Withdrawal of Motions

If you make a motion, either make sure beforehand that there is at least some support for it or be ready to stand by it if people start groaning when you make it. It does not look good to withdraw a motion just because you find out immediately after you have made it that people do not like it. If you once had a valid reason to make the motion, you still do. Let the others vote it down if they wish. On the other hand, if you can amend a seemingly unpopular motion, do that. For example, if you move for a twenty-minute caucus and people start yelling "too long," and the chair feels a ten-minute caucus would be better for the sake of debate, do not withdraw the motion; instead, ask if you can amend it to ten minutes.

Precedence

Try to know the order of precedence, but refer to your cheat sheet if you cannot memorize it all. Make sure you do not move for a point or motion when a higher-ranking one is already on the floor.

IV.   Working with Fellow Delegates

It is no secret that not every nation is equal—even though the UN is thought of as a community of equals, world realities favor some over others. However, Model UN is much closer to the idea of the community of equals. Of course, major powers have an edge by the virtue of their place in the world, but in a Model UN committee, a delegation's influence is determined by the skills of its members. A good delegate from a small island nation may have much more influence than a disinterested delegate representing a major power. Good preparation combined with debate and negotiation skills determine the status of each delegate in the committee room.

Negotiation and Diplomacy

While formal debate takes up most of the proceedings at a Model UN conference, most things get done outside of it. You need to be constantly in touch with other delegates in order to write resolutions, get support for your ideas, get yields, etc. While good preparation is a must, it is not possible to succeed without negotiation and persuasion skills as well as a good grasp of the art of compromise. There are a couple of important points that must be remembered when working with fellow delegates. First is always to show them respect and courtesy. Remember that Model UN is an educational experience; there is no need to try to humiliate or intimidate other students or to treat them in a disrespectful manner. Second is to have a diplomatic ethic. While in the real world, nations may not always stand by their word and try to profit at each other's expense, Model UN delegates should be open and honest with each other. If you do not like an idea, tell your fellow delegate; if you are not going to vote for a resolution, do not promise its authors you will. Try to convince other delegates by explaining your ideas to them in a clear manner. Show them how your ideas are beneficial to their nation, not only to yours. Be honest about what you can and cannot compromise on, and explain your position to others by convincing them that you are just doing your job of protecting your country's interests.

Blocs

Your bloc may be the best starting point to gather support for your ideas, because blocs may contain many similar viewpoints on an issue. However, it is important not to be stuck in a small group of like-minded nations. This hinders your ability to be flexible in negotiation and compromise, because you may have to make limiting commitments to your bloc. It also looks bad if delegates outside of your bloc see you as part of a clique, because they may then be less willing to work with you. It is also true that the importance of blocs has been decreasing over the last several years within the UN. Of course, there will be a core group of people that you will work with, but I suggest that you not disregard or ignore the other delegates, especially the quiet ones. Try to be in touch with as many delegations as possible, ask them their ideas, and share yours with them. Additionally, do not ignore observers. Even though they do not have a formal vote, they may have a lot of influence, and NGO representatives are often the most resourceful people in the committee.

Consensus

Following the end of the Cold War, cooperation in the UN has increased dramatically, and today the majority of General Assembly resolutions are adopted by consensus, without a formal vote. Model UN conferences encourage delegates to do the same, and I believe it is a good idea. The more support there is for a resolution, the more legitimate it will be. You should strive to get unanimous support for your ideas without jeopardizing your vital interests.

Notes

Passing notes is an excellent way of communicating with other delegations. If you use notes efficiently, you can get yields, work on amendments and resolutions, and get support for your ideas without having to wait for caucus time.

Some conferences require that delegations have official notepads. Even if this is not the case, it is a good idea as a delegation, or individually, to come prepared with papers that have the name of your nation on them and a "To:" line. Divide a letter-size document into four equal pieces on your computer and put your delegation's name and a "To:" line on each quarter. Then photocopy this sheet and divide it into fours. This will not only look professional but will also save you a lot of time at the conference. Also keep in mind that some conferences and chairs screen notes, so stick to business and save personal messages until after session is over.

Home Government

Even though nothing can match the quality of thorough research done before the conference, at many conferences, delegates can ask their "home government" for information relating to the debate when they are not sure of what policy to follow. This service is provided either by a member of the dais or by the Secretariat.

There are two types of home governments at a Model UN conference: the passive and the active. To the passive home government, delegates can make inquiries ranging from obtaining voting records to getting a copy of a past resolution. Of course, the range of information available is limited by the policies and resources of the conference. The home government can provide important information, but unless the committee is dealing with a crisis situation, I do not suggest using this service as there is nothing that you can learn from them that you could not have found out during your preconference research. Asking for such information only shows that you are ill prepared. However, the case, as I have mentioned, is different for a crisis situation. If you were not expected to have done research on a topic, then by all means try to obtain as much information from the home government as possible.

The active home government not only responds to inquiries but also actively updates the delegate with information and sometimes simulated top-secret documents, such as an intelligence report about troop movements. The home governments may sometimes alter the truth and provide not-so-pleasant information in an effort to challenge you. Take the information from your home government as given if it is meant to be fictitious. But if you ask about your nation's real policy, and the conference organizers who act as the home government provide you with information that you believe is not accurate, you may want to talk to them to make sure you are on the same page.

Additional Tactics That Will Help You

- Learn delegates' real names: it's so much better to be referred to as "Mike" than "Kenya" (after the sessions are over).
- Ask powerful countries with potential to sway votes to sponsor your resolution, even if they have not had input in it.
- Bring a laptop if you have one or borrow one; you will be able to work on resolutions without having to wait for a computer or leave the room.

- Do not bring too much research with you; it will make you look unsure of yourself.

V. Dealing with Staff Members

Although enforcing the rules of procedure may seem to delegates like the main responsibility of the chairing staff, the dais is charged with much more. Chairing staffs work with the delegates to help them write resolutions, negotiate and compromise on issues, and come to agreements. They are also responsible for involving delegates in debate by encouraging delegates to deliver speeches and to participate in caucusing and resolution writing. In applying the rules of procedure and leading debate, members of the chairing staff must be fluent in the rules of procedure as well as knowledgeable about the conference topics and international affairs in general.

An effective chair speaks with a soft yet firm voice and with authority, is fair, objective, and impartial, and has an amicable personality. The best chairs preside over the entire conference without once banging their gavels. Chairs must not cross a fine line of professional behavior, but they should still be amiable and have a sense of humor whenever possible, without being sarcastic. Good chairs know when to allow or propose caucuses and when to entertain motions. They follow the debate and caucuses closely and will lead the body in the right direction when it is veering off track.

It is easy to take a good chair for granted, and you will only know his or her value when you get an incompetent or bad-intentioned one. A few years ago, a close friend was in a large committee at a large conference. He was well prepared, represented a major nation, and was able to get a lot of support for his ideas. His main rival was another major nation with a completely different agenda. In the end, two big groups formed, each with a draft resolution. Things were going well for my friend because his group had more support and it seemed like they were going to pass their resolution—until it was rejected by the chair. The chair claimed that the resolution was too weak. Whatever changes they made, the chair was determined not to accept it. The other group's resolution was allowed to be introduced, amended heavily, and partially adopted. It turned out toward the end of the conference that my friend's rival happened to be high school friends with the chair, and they both admitted that they wrote the resolution together! You can imagine how frustrated my friend was. Although this is an unusual instance, it illustrates why you should not take a good chair for granted.

If you have a problem with your chairing staff, you should first try to discuss your problem with them. Do so politely, without making them angry. If that does not work, you can go to your head delegate or faculty advisor, who in turn can talk to the Secretariat about the problem. But make sure that what you deem as a problem is not simply a misunderstanding before you take action. For example, the chair of a committee I was in did not recognize me half as much as he should have during the first couple of sessions of the conference. I had no idea why this was happening, but it was clear that I was not getting my fair share of time. Just as I was planning to talk to him in the third session, a crisis situation was introduced, and it directly involved my nation, so until the end of the conference I got plenty of speaking time! The chair was not recognizing me on purpose in order to see my reaction, and also because he knew I would be getting a lot of speaking time later on in the conference.

I suggest that you always act in a friendly yet polite and professional manner toward your chairing staff, and that includes every single one of them, from top to bottom. Remember that they have worked hard to make your experience a pleasant one, and they deserve courtesy. If they make mistakes, try not to make a big deal out of it unless it becomes repetitive and systematic—they are human too.

Typical Phrases Used by the Chair

- "The chair recognizes the delegate from the Solomon Islands."
- "The house will come to order now."
- "There is a motion to close debate. Is there a second to this motion?"
- "Moldova has the floor for exactly three minutes."
- "I will rule a motion for caucus out of order at this time."
- "To what point do you rise, Malaysia?"
- "That is not a question, delegate; please use the point of

information to ask a question."
- "Will the delegate please repeat the point?"
- "Are there any further points or motions on the floor?"
- "Delegate, your time has expired, please take your seat."

VI.   Awards

There are many criteria in determining awards, and conferences use some or all of these and weigh them in different ways to determine awards. The following will be factors in determining awards in a committee:

- Quality and quantity of speeches, points of information, and comments
- Being consistent and on-policy
- Attendance
- Attitude and courtesy
- Contribution to resolution writing
- Leadership in committee

Some combination of these factors determines the best delegate award, as well as honorable mentions. There may be a few honorable mentions given in each committee, depending on its size. It is worth noting that being the sole author of the only resolution adopted by the committee does not guarantee an award, nor does being the only odd vote in the committee against every decision automatically exclude one from winning an award. It is the process that matters, not the outcome of a vote or even the resolution of a crisis.

As far as team awards are concerned, the overall performances of delegations determine the awards. This usually means the ratio of the number of individual awards to the overall size of the delegation, with best delegate and other awards having different weighted values in the calculation of this ratio.

As I explained in Chapter One, you do not need to win an award to benefit from Model United Nations, but if it happens, all the better.

CHAPTER SIX:
RESOLUTIONS

I.   How to Write Them

Resolutions are the main instruments used by the United Nations to take action or make policy. A resolution is what the body has to say about the topic at hand, whatever it may be, from admitting a new member to placing sanctions on a country. As such, resolutions come in a variety of forms: recommendations, opinions (usually condemnations or criticisms), treaties, conventions, and executive orders, including everything from budget appropriations to sanctions.

Most resolutions that you will write and debate during the conference will be recommendations. This is due to the very nature of the UN System, because only the Security Council, and in rare instances the General Assembly, has executive decision-making authority. Otherwise, resolutions usually place only a moral pressure on nations. The only exceptions are conventions and treaties, but those are binding only on their signatories. This system has its advantages and disadvantages for you as a Model UN delegate. It is good because it makes it easier to reach compromises and bad because your recommendation can be entirely disregarded by those for whom it is intended.

In real life, multiple resolutions, sometimes almost identical to one another, can be and will be passed by a body. Reflecting this practice, most Model UN conferences allow passing multiple resolutions on a topic.[1] However, some conferences allow only one

---

1   Some of these conferences allow a committee to decide whether to vote on other resolutions after the committee has adopted one resolution.

resolution to be passed on any single topic, with either the chairing staff deciding which resolution will be voted on or resolutions being voted on in the order in which they were submitted. When that is the case, compromise and lobbying become even more important.

Writing a resolution can be enjoyable but also frustrating. No matter how great your ideas are and how wonderful your draft resolution may be, it is practically impossible to get enough support for it in its original unamended form. Every delegate will have his or her own agenda and ideas. They will not like your word choices, find your resolution too soft, too strong, too idealistic, not determined enough—you name it. What usually happens is that working papers and speeches lead to like minds getting together to write a draft resolution. But even this does not mean things will run smoothly. There will be several voices all saying something different and possibly even fights.

If you identify each delegate's style early on, you can use that to your advantage. For example, there is the type who wants to be the star. He or she will want to be the one typing the resolution, the one coming up with the actual clauses, the one schmoozing to the dais, and the one trying to neutralize strong delegates. He or she will be annoying, manipulative, and a pain to work with. This type of delegate will run to the dais every five minutes, asking questions, telling them how he or she has great ideas about the topic and how his or her resolution is being typed as they speak. But here is the good news: you do not have to work with that delegate. In fact, it will probably be to your advantage not to work with this type of delegate—remember this: every delegation has one vote and they, exceptions notwithstanding, all count the same. By and large, chairs frown upon such delegates.

Then there are also the delegates who are resourceful, speak only as much as necessary, and are ready to compromise. They are the best ones to work with. They are straightforward, always tell you what they think, and when they see the same sincerity in you, they will offer their help and knowledge.

Yet another type is what I like to call the "disinterested delegate," who hardly ever speaks, may even skip sessions, and when he or she does attend them, looks completely bored in the back row. Ask them what they think about the topic and your ideas. Ask them to give you input and get their support. This type of delegate may be the most willing to sign your draft resolution. Remember, resolutions are usually recommendations and not binding international law. So the higher the support for a resolution, the higher its moral pressure—unanimity is, of course, the best alternative.

Important Points in Writing a Resolution

I find the following points valuable to keep in mind when writing a resolution. The list is, of course, not exhaustive, but should provide a good starting point:

- The language must be formal, yet clear, unambiguous, and easy to understand.
- Every word and clause must be there for a reason.
- The resolution must not go off topic—keep it relevant to the issue at hand.
- Shorter clauses are easier to understand, explain, work with, amend, and compromise on.
- Have a mix of details and general clauses, and ambitious and innocuous recommendations to appeal to a broad audience.
- Try to formulate your own clauses, but it is fine to be influenced by and to borrow from past UN documents as long as you have a legitimate purpose in doing so and you understand the original text fully.
- Peaceful means are always preferable to nonpeaceful measures.
- The preambulatory clauses should not recommend anything but only give a background account of the issue.
- Cite past UN resolutions, actions, and treaties whenever possible. Respect these because it is generally not a good idea to reverse or conflict with them.
- Bring concrete and feasible solutions and suggestions, and do not ramble on. When suggesting action, talk about the funding, means, purpose, and other related themes. For example, if you are forming a new body such as an ad hoc working group, a standing committee, or a new commission, make sure you

designate the membership structure of the body, as well as its mission, mandate, and funding.

- Be as objective and impartial as possible to the maximum extent permitted by the situation—remember this is a universal document.
- Be open-minded to other viewpoints—remember this is an international effort.

Compromise

It is almost impossible for a single delegation to persuade the entire body to pass a resolution that contains all of the clauses that particular delegation likes with no clauses that it dislikes. Thus, compromise is necessary. This does not mean, however, acting off policy or jeopardizing your nation's principles. Compromise means amending and combining resolutions in such a way as to produce a coherent, logical, and effective document that is acceptable to your nation and to a majority of others.

Unfortunately, this strategy may not always work, especially on controversial topics, because each delegation has its own agenda. You can debate a topic or a resolution forever, propose changes to it, amend it, combine resolutions, amend it again, but end up not passing anything—and this is fine. It is the process that matters. Model UN is a learning experience with an element of reality in it, and as long as you make best use of the experience, the actual outcome of the vote is not so important. This is not to say that resolutions do not matter. Of course they do, but it is better to go through an intense period of debate, negotiation, and lobbying than simply pass a resolution for the sake of passing it.

Even though compromise and cooperation are necessary in resolution writing, you should nevertheless write several operative clauses on the topics before you come to the conference. Write a whole range of them, from simple, neutral ones to more radical actions. They will come in handy in writing resolutions and amending them with fellow delegates, as well as when making speeches.

"Decides to remain ..."

You may have seen that the Security Council usually ends its resolutions with the strangely worded clause "Decides to remain seized of the matter." If you wonder what this clause means and why it appears in Security Council resolutions and is not used by the other organs of the UN, there is a historical reason. While it is true that the General Assembly normally cannot take definitive action, there is one exception to this rule. The GA adopted a resolution in November 1950 called "Uniting for Peace,"[2] which gives the GA the authority to consider and to take collective action in a threatening situation or to restore international peace and security in instances when the Security Council fails to act on the matter or has simply lost interest in it. This resolution was passed at a time when there were major differences of opinion among the permanent members, and vetoes were being frequently used to block resolutions. Since the Security Council is the primary organ of the UN charged with preserving international peace and security, as long as the Security Council adds this legalistic clause to a resolution, the General Assembly cannot discuss the topic.

Draft Resolutions

Some conferences accept draft resolution submissions from delegations prior to the conference. Some conferences also write their own draft resolutions beforehand. These resolutions are then distributed and debated at the conference, provided a certain number of signatories is secured from among the participants. This method imitates the practice of writing resolutions behind the scenes, before the actual meeting, as it often occurs in the real UN. If a conference accepts draft resolutions, it is a good idea to submit one. You should already have a list of operative clauses to use at the conference. Spend some more time on them and put some clauses together in a coherent and effective manner to form a draft resolution, and then submit it.

---

2   UN General Assembly, Fifth Session, Resolution 377 (V), A/RES/377 (V), November 3, 1950.

Working Papers

Working papers are the easiest way to get ideas on the floor in a written form. They provide the basis for debate and resolution writing. Because you do not have to worry too much about formatting and need not provide a comprehensive solution, getting working papers onto the floor is relatively painless. Depending on the reactions of other delegates, you can write a generally acceptable resolution based on your working paper. Some conferences allow working papers to be submitted before the conference.

Amendments

Amendments are a great way to gain more support for a resolution without having to write it again from scratch. You should use amendments in a positive fashion, working to make a resolution stronger, not weaker. If you do not like a resolution, your speeches and lobbying should be your only weapons against it, not amendments to kill it. This applies not only because of diplomatic ethics but also for the practical reason to avoid getting tied down with too many amendments that will hinder debate. There will be tons of amendments on the floor anyway, most of them well-intentioned. It will take hours to debate and vote on these, and eventually only a few will ever be adopted. The best way to amend resolutions is during caucus, by means of negotiation and compromise, and then to present the resulting document formally in the shape of an amendment already acceptable to the majority of the committee. Friendly amendments, when in order, should be used whenever possible. This method of amending a resolution is better for the sake of debate and makes everyone's life easier.

II.   Format

Even though content determines the effectiveness and strength of a resolution, format is extremely important as well. Technically, a resolution is a single sentence, with the only full stop appearing at the very end. Everything else is separated by semicolons and commas.

There are three main components of a resolution: the heading, the preamble, and the operative clauses. This is the format that real UN bodies use. Lines are single-spaced except for a double space between clauses. Clauses always begin with a capital letter. Some conferences also number each line in the margin.

The heading of the resolution contains the name of the committee, the topic, resolution number, and, if allowed, lists the sponsoring and signatory nations.

The preamble section, otherwise called the preambulatory clauses, refers to the background and facts of the topic, past resolutions, actions, and events. The language is by and large soft and typically uses the present participle form. Preambles are important because they give background information and state the purpose of the resolution. The preamble is not debatable and cannot be amended. For this reason it is imperative that no controversial or disputable clauses be used in writing this section. Preambulatory clauses are indented and end with commas.

The main section of the resolution contains the operative clauses, which are also called the activating or actuating clauses. This is the policy, action, or opinion section. Although you will typically have more than one clause, each dealing with a single aspect, all clauses are supposed to follow a logical pattern and make sense as a whole. Each clause begins with an action verb (or an adverb plus a verb) in the third person singular, indented and underlined (real UN style is to use italics). Subclauses are lettered (a, b, c, etc.) and sub-subclauses are numbered (i, ii, iii, etc.). If using acronyms or abbreviations, write them out in full and defined them the first time you use them. Each operative clause ends with a semicolon except for the last clause, which ends with a full stop.

Preambulatory Clauses

While not an exhaustive list, preambulatory clauses typically start with the following words, which may be italicized (real UN style) or underlined, depending on the conference.

… also	Desiring	Noting
… further	Determined	Noting with appreciation
… in particular	Determining	Noting with approval
Acknowledging	Disturbed	Noting with deep concern
Acting under	Emphasizing	Noting with grave concern
Affirming	Encouraged	Noting with great concern
Alarmed	Endorsing	Noting with regret
Also …	Expecting	Noting with satisfaction
Anxious	Expressing	Observing
Appreciating	Fulfilling	Pointing out
Approving	Fully alarmed	Profoundly deploring
Aware	Fully aware	Reaffirming
Bearing in mind	Fully bearing in mind	Realizing
Being convinced	Fully believing	Recalling
Believing	Further …	Recognizing
Cognizant	Grieved	Referring
Concerned	Guided by	Regarding
Confident	Having adopted	Regretting
Congratulating	Having approved	Reiterating
Conscious	Having considered	Reminding
Considering	Having decided	Seeking
Contemplating	Having devoted attention	Seriously concerned
Convinced	Having examined	Stressing
Declaring	Having heard	Taking into account
Deeply concerned	Having received	Taking into consideration
Deeply conscious	Having regard for	Taking note
Deeply convinced	Having reviewed	Viewing with appreciation
Deeply disturbed	Having studied	Viewing with apprehension
Deeply regretting	Keeping in mind	Welcoming
Defines	Looking forward to	
Deploring	Mindful	

Operative Clauses

Here are some words that typically begin operative clauses, but you can use other ones too.

… also	Designates	Proposes
… further	Directs	Reaffirms
… in particular	Draws attention	Reaffirms its belief
Accepts	Emphasizes	Recognizes
Adopts	Encourages	Recommends
Affirms	Endorses	Regrets
Also …	Expresses	Reiterates
Appeals	Expresses its appreciation	Reminds
Appreciates	Expresses its concern	Renews its appeal
Approves	Expresses its conviction	Repeats
Asks	Expresses its regret	Reproaches
Authorizes	Expresses its solidarity	Requests
Calls	Expresses its sympathy	Resolves
Calls for	Expresses its thanks	Seeks
Calls upon	Expresses the belief	Solemnly affirms
Commends	Expresses the hope	Stresses
Concurs	Further …	Strongly condemns
Condemns	Has resolved	Strongly requests
Confirms	Hopes	Strongly urges
Congratulates	Instructs	Suggests
Considers	Invites	Supports
Declares	Notes	Transmits
Declares accordingly	Notes with appreciation	Trusts
Decides	Notes with approval	Urges
Decides accordingly	Notes with interest	Welcomes
Demands	Notes with satisfaction	
Deplores	Proclaims	

III. Sample Resolutions

The following resolutions are real UN resolutions. The first resolution, on the Comprehensive Nuclear Test-Ban Treaty, is Resolution 55/41 adopted by the General Assembly on November 20, 2000 in its 69th plenary meeting during its 55th session, on the report of the First Committee. The second resolution is on human rights and terrorism, and was adopted by the General Assembly as Resolution 54/164 on December 17, 1999 in its 83rd plenary meeting during its 54th session, on the report of the Third Committee. The third and last resolution, on the situation between Eritrea and Ethiopia, was adopted by the Security Council in its 4,144th meeting on May 17, 2000 as Resolution 1298. While the texts of the documents were untouched, the headings were altered to fit the Model UN format for the purposes of this book.

Sample Resolution 1

Resolution: 1.1
Committee: Disarmament and International Security
Topic Area: Comprehensive Nuclear-Test-Ban Treaty

The General Assembly,

Recalling that the Comprehensive Nuclear-Test-Ban Treaty was adopted by its resolution 50/245 of 10 September 1996 and opened for signature on 24 September 1996,

Noting that, in its resolution 54/63 of 1 December 1999, it decided to include in the provisional agenda of its fifty-fifth session the item entitled "Comprehensive Nuclear-Test-Ban Treaty,"

Encouraged by the signing of the Treaty by one hundred and sixty States, including forty-one of the forty-four needed for its entry into force, and welcoming the ratification of sixty-five States, including thirty of the forty-four needed for its entry into force,

Recalling its endorsement, in resolution 54/63, of the Final Declaration of the Conference on Facilitating the Entry into Force of the Comprehensive Nuclear-Test-Ban Treaty,[1] held at Vienna from 6 to 8 October 1999 to promote the entry into force of the Treaty at the earliest possible date,

1. Stresses the importance and urgency of signature and ratification, without delay and without conditions and in accordance with constitutional processes, to achieve the early entry into force of the Comprehensive Nuclear-Test-Ban Treaty;

2. Welcomes the contributions by the States signatories to the work of the Preparatory Commission for the Comprehensive Nuclear-Test-Ban Treaty Organization, in particular to its efforts to ensure that the Treaty's verification regime will be capable of meeting the verification requirements of the Treaty upon its entry into force, in accordance with article IV of the Treaty;

3. Urges States to maintain their moratoria on nuclear weapons test explosions or any other nuclear explosions, pending the entry into force of the Treaty;

4. Calls upon all States that have not yet signed the Treaty to sign and ratify it as soon as possible and to refrain from acts that would defeat its object and purpose in the meanwhile;

5. Calls upon all States that have signed but not yet ratified the Treaty, in particular those whose ratification is needed for its entry into force, to accelerate their ratification processes with a view to their early successful conclusion;

6. Urges all States to remain seized of the issue at the highest political level;

7. Decides to include in the provisional agenda of its fifty-sixth session the item entitled "Comprehensive Nuclear-Test-Ban Treaty".

---

(1) A/54/514-S/1999/1102, annex.

Sample Resolution 2

Resolution: 2.1
Committee: Social, Humanitarian and Cultural
Topic Area: Human Rights and Terrorism

The General Assembly,

Guided by the Charter of the United Nations, the Universal Declaration of Human Rights,[1] the Declaration on Principles of International Law concerning Friendly Relations and Cooperation among States in accordance with the Charter of the United Nations[2] and the International Covenants on Human Rights,[3]

Recalling the Declaration on the Occasion of the Fiftieth Anniversary of the United Nations,[4]

Recalling also the Vienna Declaration and Programme of Action adopted by the World Conference on Human Rights on 25 June 1993,[5] in which the Conference reaffirmed that terrorism is indeed aimed at the destruction of human rights, fundamental freedoms and democracy,

Recalling further its resolutions 48/122 of 20 December 1993, 49/185 of 23 December 1994, 50/186 of 22 December 1995 and 52/133 of 12 December 1997,

Recalling in particular its resolution 52/133, in which it requested the Secretary-General to seek the views of Member States on the implications of terrorism, in all its forms and manifestations, for the full enjoyment of human rights and fundamental freedoms,

Recalling previous resolutions of the Commission on Human Rights, and taking note, in particular, of resolution 1999/27 of 26 April 1999,[6] as well as the relevant resolutions of the Subcommission on the Promotion and Protection of Human Rights,[7]

Alarmed that acts of terrorism in all its forms and manifestations aimed at the destruction of human rights have continued despite national and international efforts,

Bearing in mind that the essential and most basic human right is the right to life,

Bearing in mind also that terrorism creates an environment that destroys the right of people to live in freedom from fear,

Reiterating that all States have an obligation to promote and protect all human rights and fundamental freedoms and that every individual should strive to secure their universal and effective recognition and observance,

Seriously concerned about the gross violations of human rights perpetrated by terrorist groups,

Profoundly deploring the increasing number of innocent persons, including women, children and the elderly, killed, massacred and maimed by terrorists in indiscriminate and random acts of violence and terror, which cannot be justified under any circumstances,

Noting with great concern the growing connection between the terrorist groups and other criminal organizations engaged in the illegal traffic in arms and drugs at the national and international levels, as well as the consequent commission of serious crimes such as murder, extortion, kidnapping, assault, the taking of hostages and robbery,

Emphasizing the importance of Member States taking appropriate steps to deny safe haven to those who plan, finance or commit terrorist acts, by ensuring their apprehension and prosecution or extradition,

Mindful of the need to protect the human rights of and guarantees for the individual in accordance with the relevant human rights principles and instruments, in particular the right to life,

Reaffirming that all measures to counter terrorism must be in strict conformity with the relevant provisions of international law including international human rights standards,

1. Expresses its solidarity with the victims of terrorism;

2. Condemns the violations of the right to live free from fear and of the right to life, liberty and security;

3. Reiterates its unequivocal condemnation of the acts, methods and practices of terrorism, in all its forms and manifestations, as activities aimed at the destruction of human rights, fundamental freedoms and democracy, threatening the territorial integrity and security of States, destabilizing legitimately constituted Governments, undermining pluralistic civil society and having adverse consequences for the economic and social development of States;

4. Calls upon States to take all necessary and effective measures in accordance with relevant provisions of international law, including international human rights standards, to prevent, combat and eliminate terrorism in all its forms and manifestations, wherever and by whomever committed;

5. Urges the international community to enhance cooperation at the regional and international levels in the fight against terrorism, in accordance with relevant international instruments, including those relating to human rights, with the aim of its eradication;

6. Condemns the incitement of ethnic hatred, violence and terrorism;

7. Commends those Governments that have communicated their views on the implications of terrorism in response to the note verbale by the Secretary-General dated 16 August 1999;

8. Welcomes the report of the Secretary-General,[8] and requests him to continue to seek the views of Member States on the implications of terrorism, in all its forms and manifestations, for the full enjoyment of all human rights and fundamental freedoms, with a view to incorporating them in his report;

9. <u>Decides</u> to consider this question at its fifty-sixth session, under the item entitled "Human rights questions".

_____

(1) Resolution 217 A (III).
(2) Resolution 2625 (XXV), annex.
(3) Resolution 2200 A (XXI), annex.
(4) See resolution 50/6.
(5) A/CONF.157/24 (Part I), chap. III.
(6) See Official Records of the Economic and Social Council, 1999, Supplement No. 3 (E/1999/23), chap. II, sect. A.
(7) Formerly known as the Subcommission on Prevention of Discrimination and Protection of Minorities.
(8) A/54/439.

Sample Resolution 3

Resolution: 3.1
Committee: Security Council
Topic Area: The Situation between Eritrea and Ethiopia

The Security Council,

Recalling its resolutions 1177 (1998) of 26 June 1998, 1226 (1999) of 29 January 1999, 1227 (1999) of 10 February 1999 and 1297 (2000) of 12 May 2000,

Recalling in particular its urging of all States to end all sales of arms and munitions to Eritrea and Ethiopia contained in its resolution 1227 (1999),

Deeply disturbed by the continuation of fighting between Eritrea and Ethiopia,

Deploring the loss of human life resulting from the fighting, and strongly regretting the negative impact the diversion of resources to the conflict continues to have on efforts to address the ongoing humanitarian food crisis in the region,

Stressing the need for both parties to achieve a peaceful resolution of the conflict,

Reaffirming the commitment of all Member States to the sovereignty, independence and territorial integrity of Eritrea and Ethiopia,

Expressing its strong support for the efforts of the Organization of African Unity (OAU) to achieve a peaceful resolution of the conflict,

Noting that the proximity talks held in Algiers from 29 April to 5 May 2000 and reported in the OAU Communiqué of 5 May 2000 (S/2000/394) were intended to assist the two parties to arrive at a final detailed peace implementation plan acceptable to each of them, which would lead to the peaceful resolution of the conflict,

Recalling the efforts of the Security Council, including through its Mission to the region, to achieve a peaceful resolution of the situation,

Convinced of the need for further and immediate diplomatic efforts,

Noting with concern that the fighting has serious humanitarian implications for the civilian population of the two States,

Stressing that the hostilities constitute an increasing threat to the stability, security and economic development of the subregion,

Determining that the situation between Eritrea and Ethiopia constitutes a threat to regional peace and security,

Acting under Chapter VII of the Charter of the United Nations,

1. <u>Strongly condemns</u> the continued fighting between Eritrea and Ethiopia;

2. <u>Demands</u> that both parties immediately cease all military action and refrain from the further use of force;

3. <u>Demands further</u> that both parties withdraw their forces from military engagement and take no action that would aggravate tensions;

4. <u>Demands</u> the earliest possible reconvening, without preconditions, of substantive peace talks, under OAU auspices, on the basis of the Framework Agreement and the Modalities and of the work conducted by the OAU as recorded in its Communiqué issued by its current Chairman of 5 May 2000 (S/2000/394), which would conclude a peaceful definitive settlement of the conflict;

5. <u>Requests</u> that the current Chairman of the OAU consider dispatching urgently his Personal Envoy to the region to seek immediate cessation of hostilities and resumption of the peace talks;

6. <u>Decides</u> that all States shall prevent:

(a) the sale or supply to Eritrea and Ethiopia, by their nationals or from their territories, or using their flag vessels or aircraft, of arms and related matériel of all types, including weapons and ammunition, military vehicles and equipment, paramilitary equipment and spare parts for the aforementioned, whether or not originating in their territory;

(b) any provision to Eritrea and Ethiopia by their nationals or from their territories of technical assistance or training related to the provision, manufacture, maintenance or use of the items in (a) above;

7. <u>Decides also</u> that the measures imposed by paragraph 6 above shall not apply to supplies of non-lethal military equipment intended solely for humanitarian use, as approved in advance by the Committee established by paragraph 8 below;

8. <u>Decides</u> to establish, in accordance with rule 28 of its provisional rules of procedure, a Committee of the Security Council consisting of all the members of the Council, to undertake the following tasks and to report on its work to the Council with its observations and recommendations:

(a) to seek from all States further information regarding the action taken by them with a view to implementing effectively the measures imposed by paragraph 6 above, and thereafter to request from them whatever further information it may consider necessary;

(b) to consider information brought to its attention by States concerning violations of the measures imposed by paragraph 6 above and to recommend appropriate measures in response thereto;

(c) to make periodic reports to the Security Council on information submitted to it regarding alleged violations of the measures imposed by paragraph 6 above, identifying where possible persons or entities, including vessels and aircraft, reported to be engaged in such violations;

(d) to promulgate such guidelines as may be necessary to facilitate the implementation of the measures imposed by paragraph 6 above;

(e) to give consideration to, and decide upon, requests for the exceptions set out in paragraph 7 above;

(f) to examine the reports submitted pursuant to paragraphs 11 and 12 below;

9. Calls upon all States and all international and regional organizations to act strictly in conformity with this resolution, notwithstanding the existence of any rights granted or obligations conferred or imposed by any international agreement or of any contract entered into or any licence or permit granted prior to the entry into force of the measures imposed by paragraph 6 above;

10. Requests the Secretary-General to provide all necessary assistance to the Committee established by paragraph 8 above and to make the necessary arrangements in the Secretariat for this purpose;

11. Requests States to report in detail to the Secretary-General within 30 days of the date of adoption of this resolution on the

specific steps they have taken to give effect to the measures imposed by paragraph 6 above;

12. Requests all States, relevant United Nations bodies and, as appropriate, other organizations and interested parties to report information on possible violations of the measures imposed by paragraph 6 above to the Committee established by paragraph 8 above;

13. Requests the Committee established by paragraph 8 above to make information it considers relevant publicly available through appropriate media, including through the improved use of information technology;

14. Requests the Governments of Eritrea and Ethiopia and other concerned parties to establish appropriate arrangements for the provision of humanitarian assistance and to endeavour to ensure that such assistance responds to local needs and is safely delivered to, and used by, its intended recipients;

15. Requests the Secretary-General to submit an initial report to the Council within 15 days of the date of adoption of this resolution on compliance with paragraphs 2, 3 and 4 above, and thereafter every 60 days after the date of adoption of this resolution on its implementation and on the humanitarian situation in Eritrea and Ethiopia;

16. Decides that the measures imposed by paragraph 6 above are established for twelve months and that, at the end of this period, the Council will decide whether the Governments of Eritrea and Ethiopia have complied with paragraphs 2, 3 and 4 above, and, accordingly, whether to extend these measures for a further period with the same conditions;

17. Decides also that the measures imposed by paragraph 6 above shall be terminated immediately if the Secretary-General reports that a peaceful definitive settlement of the conflict has been concluded;

18. Decides to remain seized of the matter.

Appendix A:

Members and Permanent Observers of the United Nations

For the most current list of members and permanent observers, as well as contact information for each permanent mission, you can download the *Blue Book* available on the website of the United Nations Protocol and Liaison Service at http://www.un.int/protocol.

I.   Member Nations

Regional Groups: Regional groups are informal caucusing groups. These groups are also used to divide members into voting blocs for voting purposes, but members of a regional group are in no way required to vote in a certain way; the division is only for procedural purposes. The presidency of the General Assembly rotates among the regional groups. The five regional groups are:

- African States (fifty-three members)
- Asian States (fifty-four members, one of which is not part of the group for voting purposes)
- Eastern European States (twenty-three members)
- Latin American and Caribbean States (GRULAC) (thirty-three members)
- Western European and Other States (WEOG) (twenty-seven full members plus one member with limited participation)

Nation	Date of Admission	Group
Afghanistan	19 November 1946	Asian
Albania	14 December 1955	Eastern European
Algeria	8 October 1962	African
Andorra	28 July 1993	WEOG
Angola	1 December 1976	African
Antigua and Barbuda	11 November 1981	GRULAC
Argentina	24 October 1945	GRULAC
Armenia	2 March 1992	Eastern European
Australia	1 November 1945	WEOG
Austria	14 December 1955	WEOG
Azerbaijan	2 March 1992	Eastern European
Bahamas	18 September 1973	GRULAC
Bahrain	21 September 1971	Asian
Bangladesh	17 September 1974	Asian
Barbados	9 December 1966	GRULAC
Belarus[1]	24 October 1945	Eastern European
Belgium	27 December 1945	WEOG
Belize	25 September 1981	GRULAC
Benin	20 September 1960	African
Bhutan	21 September 1971	Asian
Bolivia	14 November 1945	GRULAC
Bosnia and Herzegovina[2]	22 May 1992	Eastern European
Botswana	17 October 1966	African
Brazil	24 October 1945	GRULAC
Brunei Darussalam	21 September 1984	Asian
Bulgaria	14 December 1955	Eastern European
Burkina Faso	20 September 1960	African
Burundi	18 September 1962	African
Cambodia	14 December 1955	Asian
Cameroon	20 September 1960	African
Canada	9 November 1945	WEOG

Nation	Date of Admission	Group
Cape Verde	16 September 1975	African
Central African Republic	20 September 1960	African
Chad	20 September 1960	African
Chile	24 October 1945	GRULAC
China	24 October 1945	Asian
Colombia	5 November 1945	GRULAC
Comoros	12 November 1975	African
Congo, Republic of the	20 September 1960	African
Costa Rica	2 November 1945	GRULAC
Côte d'Ivoire	20 September 1960	African
Croatia[2]	22 May 1992	Eastern European
Cuba	24 October 1945	GRULAC
Cyprus	20 September 1960	Asian
Czech Republic[3]	19 January 1993	Eastern European
Democratic People's Republic of Korea	17 September 1991	Asian
Democratic Republic of the Congo[4]	20 September 1960	African
Denmark	24 October 1945	WEOG
Djibouti	20 September 1977	African
Dominica	18 December 1978	GRULAC
Dominican Republic	24 October 1945	GRULAC
Ecuador	21 December 1945	GRULAC
Egypt[5]	24 October 1945	African
El Salvador	24 October 1945	GRULAC
Equatorial Guinea	12 November 1968	African
Eritrea	28 May 1993	African
Estonia	17 September 1991	Eastern European
Ethiopia	13 November 1945	African
Fiji	13 October 1970	Asian
Finland	14 December 1955	WEOG
France	24 October 1945	WEOG

Nation	Date of Admission	Group
Gabon	20 September 1960	African
Gambia	21 September 1965	African
Georgia	31 July 1992	Eastern European
Germany[6]	18 September 1973	WEOG
Ghana	8 March 1957	African
Greece	25 October 1945	WEOG
Grenada	17 September 1974	GRULAC
Guatemala	21 November 1945	GRULAC
Guinea	12 December 1958	African
Guinea-Bissau	17 September 1974	African
Guyana	20 September 1966	GRULAC
Haiti	24 October 1945	GRULAC
Honduras	17 December 1945	GRULAC
Hungary	14 December 1955	Eastern European
Iceland	19 November 1946	WEOG
India	30 October 1945	Asian
Indonesia[7]	28 September 1950	Asian
Iran, Islamic Republic of	24 October 1945	Asian
Iraq	21 December 1945	Asian
Ireland	14 December 1955	WEOG
Israel	11 May 1949	WEOG [8]
Italy	14 December 1955	WEOG
Jamaica	18 September 1962	GRULAC
Japan	18 December 1956	Asian
Jordan	14 December 1955	Asian
Kazakhstan	2 March 1992	Asian
Kenya	16 December 1963	African
Kiribati	14 September 1999	——[9]
Kuwait	14 May 1963	Asian
Kyrgyzstan	2 March 1992	Asian
Lao People's Democratic Republic	14 December 1955	Asian

Nation	Date of Admission	Group
Latvia	17 September 1991	Eastern European
Lebanon	24 October 1945	Asian
Lesotho	17 October 1966	African
Liberia	2 November 1945	African
Libyan Arab Jamahiriya	14 December 1955	African
Liechtenstein	18 September 1990	WEOG
Lithuania	17 September 1991	Eastern European
Luxembourg	24 October 1945	WEOG
Macedonia, the former Yugoslav Republic of[2]	8 April 1993	Eastern European
Madagascar	20 September 1960	African
Malawi	1 December 1964	African
Malaysia[10]	17 September 1957	Asian
Maldives	21 September 1965	Asian
Mali	28 September 1960	African
Malta	1 December 1964	WEOG
Marshall Islands	17 September 1991	Asian
Mauritania	27 October 1961	African
Mauritius	24 April 1968	African
Mexico	7 November 1945	GRULAC
Micronesia, Federated States of	17 September 1991	Asian
Moldova	2 March 1992	Eastern European
Monaco	28 May 1993	WEOG
Mongolia	27 October 1961	Asian
Montenegro[2]	28 June 2006	Eastern European
Morocco	12 November 1956	African
Mozambique	16 September 1975	African
Myanmar	19 April 1948	Asian
Namibia	23 April 1990	African
Nauru	14 September 1999	Asian
Nepal	14 December 1955	Asian

Nation	Date of Admission	Group
Netherlands	10 December 1945	WEOG
New Zealand	24 October 1945	WEOG
Nicaragua	24 October 1945	GRULAC
Niger	20 September 1960	African
Nigeria	7 October 1960	African
Norway	27 November 1945	WEOG
Oman	7 October 1971	Asian
Pakistan	30 September 1947	Asian
Palau	15 December 1994	Asian
Panama	13 November 1945	GRULAC
Papua New Guinea	10 October 1975	Asian
Paraguay	24 October 1945	GRULAC
Peru	31 October 1945	GRULAC
Philippines	24 October 1945	Asian
Poland	24 October 1945	Eastern European
Portugal	14 December 1955	WEOG
Qatar	21 September 1971	Asian
Republic of Korea	17 September 1991	Asian
Romania	14 December 1955	Eastern European
Russian Federation[11]	24 October 1945	Eastern European
Rwanda	18 September 1962	African
Saint Kitts and Nevis	23 September 1983	GRULAC
Saint Lucia	18 September 1979	GRULAC
Saint Vincent and the Grenadines	16 September 1980	GRULAC
Samoa	15 December 1976	Asian
San Marino	2 March 1992	WEOG
Sao Tome and Principe	16 September 1975	African
Saudi Arabia	24 October 1945	Asian
Senegal	28 September 1960	African
Serbia[2]	1 November 2000	Eastern European
Seychelles	21 September 1976	African

Nation	Date of Admission	Group
Sierra Leone	27 September 1961	African
Singapore[12]	21 September 1965	Asian
Slovakia[3]	19 January 1993	Eastern European
Slovenia[2]	22 May 1992	Eastern European
Solomon Islands	19 September 1978	Asian
Somalia	20 September 1960	African
South Africa	7 November 1945	African
Spain	14 December 1955	WEOG
Sri Lanka	14 December 1955	Asian
Sudan	12 November 1956	African
Suriname	4 December 1975	GRULAC
Swaziland	24 September 1968	African
Sweden	19 November 1946	WEOG
Switzerland	10 September 2002	WEOG
Syrian Arab Republic[5]	24 October 1945	Asian
Tajikistan	2 March 1992	Asian
Thailand	16 December 1946	Asian
Timor-Leste	27 September 2002	Asian
Togo	20 September 1960	African
Tonga	14 September 1999	Asian
Trinidad and Tobago	18 September 1962	GRULAC
Tunisia	12 November 1956	African
Turkey	24 October 1945	WEOG[13]
Turkmenistan	2 March 1992	Asian
Tuvalu	5 September 2000	Asian
Uganda	25 October 1962	African
Ukraine	24 October 1945	Eastern European
United Arab Emirates	9 December 1971	Asian
United Kingdom of Great Britain and Northern Ireland	24 October 1945	WEOG

Nation	Date of Admission	Group
United Republic of Tanzania[14]	14 December 1961	African
United States of America	24 October 1945	———[15]
Uruguay	18 December 1945	GRULAC
Uzbekistan	2 March 1992	Asian
Vanuatu	15 September 1981	Asian
Venezuela, Bolivarian Republic of	15 November 1945	GRULAC
Viet Nam	20 September 1977	Asian
Yemen[16]	30 September 1947	Asian
Zambia	1 December 1964	African
Zimbabwe	25 August 1980	African

Original fifty-one members: Argentina, Australia, Belgium, Brazil, Bolivia, Belarus, Canada, Chile, China, Colombia, Costa Rica, Cuba, Czechoslovakia, Denmark, Dominican Republic, Ecuador, Egypt, El Salvador, Ethiopia, France, Greece, Guatemala, Haiti, Honduras, India, Iran, Iraq, Lebanon, Liberia, Luxembourg, Mexico, Netherlands, New Zealand, Nicaragua, Norway, Panama, Paraguay, Peru, Philippines, Poland, Saudi Arabia, South Africa, Syrian Arab Republic, Turkey, Ukraine, United Kingdom, United States of America, Uruguay, Union of Soviet Socialist Republics, Venezuela, Yugoslavia.

---

(1) Byelorussia changed its name to Belarus in 1991.

(2) After the breakup of the Socialist Federal Republic of Yugoslavia (an original member) in 1992, the newly formed states of Bosnia and Herzegovina, the Republic of Croatia, the Republic of Slovenia, The Former Yugoslav Republic of Macedonia, and the Federal Republic of Yugoslavia were admitted as members of the UN. In 2003, the Federal Republic of Yugoslavia changed its name to Serbia and Montenegro. In 2006, the membership of Serbia and Montenegro was assumed by Serbia, following Montenegro's declaration of independence.

(3) After the splitting up of Czechoslovakia (an original member) into the Czech Republic and the Slovak Republic, both nations were admitted as member states.

(4) Zaire changed its name to the Democratic Republic of the Congo in 1997.

(5) Egypt and Syria, both original members, united in 1958 to form the United Arab

Republic (UAR). Syria broke away from the UAR and resumed its independent status within the UN beginning in 1961. The UAR changed its name to the Arab Republic of Egypt in 1971.

(6) The Federal Republic of Germany (West Germany) and the German Democratic Republic (East Germany) became members on 18 September 1973. After the unification of the two countries, the Federal Republic of Germany continued as a single member from 3 October 1990.

(7) On 20 January 1965, Indonesia announced its decision to withdraw from the United Nations. On 19 September 1966, it announced its decision to resume its participation and on 28 September 1966, the President of the General Assembly invited Indonesia to resume its seat in the General Assembly.

(8) Israel is a member of the WEOG for election purposes in New York.

(9) Kiribati is not a member of any regional group as of 2006. Prior to that, it was a member of the Asian States group.

(10) Originally admitted as the Federation of Malaya on 17 September 1957, the country's name was changed in 1963 to Malaysia after Singapore, Sabah (North Borneo) and Sarawak became parts of the Federation. Singapore gained its independence in 1965 and became a UN member on 21 September 1965.

(11) In 1991, the Russian Federation assumed the seat of the Union of Soviet Socialist Republics (an original member) after the break-up of that country.

(12) Singapore was originally admitted as part of Malaysia. It gained its independence in 1965 and became a UN member on 21 September 1965.

(13) Turkey is a full member of both the Asian States and WEOG groups, but for voting purposes it is a member of the WEOG only.

(14) Tanganyika and Zanzibar (admitted on 14 December 1961 and 16 December 1963, respectively) formed the United Republic of Tanganyika and Zanzibar on 26 April 1964 and became a single member. On 1 November 1964, the name was changed to the United Republic of Tanzania.

(15) The United States is not an official member of any regional group. It attends meetings of the WEOG as an observer and is considered a member of the WEOG for voting purposes.

(16) Yemen and Democratic Yemen (admitted on 30 September 1947 and 14 December 1967, respectively) united on 22 May 1990 and are now represented as a single member as Yemen.

II.   Permanent Observers

Nonmember States with Permanent Missions

The Holy See (Vatican) is currently the only nonmember state with a standing invitation to participate as an observer in the General Assembly and maintain a permanent observer mission at the UN headquarters.

Entities with Permanent Missions

Palestine is currently the only "entity" with a standing invitation to participate as an observer in the General Assembly and maintain a permanent observer mission at the UN headquarters.

Intergovernmental Organizations

The following intergovernmental organizations have received standing invitations to participate as observers in the General Assembly and maintain permanent observer offices at the UN headquarters:

- African Union
- Asian-African Legal Consultative Organization
- Caribbean Community
- Central American Integration System
- Commonwealth Secretariat
- Cooperation Council for the Arab States of the Gulf
- European Community
- International Criminal Court
- International Criminal Police Organization (INTERPOL)
- International Development Law Organization
- International Institute for Democracy and Electoral Assistance
- International Organization for Migration
- International Organization of la Francophonie
- International Seabed Authority
- International Tribunal for the Law of the Sea
- International Union for the Conservation of Nature and Natural Resources
- League of Arab States
- Organisation of the Islamic Conference
- Partners in Population and Development

The following intergovernmental organizations have received standing invitations to participate as observers in the General Assembly but *do not* maintain permanent observer offices at the UN headquarters:

- African, Caribbean and Pacific Group of States
- African Development Bank
- Agency for the Prohibition of Nuclear Weapons in Latin America and the Caribbean
- Andean Community
- Asian Development Bank
- Association of Caribbean States
- Association of Southeast Asian Nations
- Black Sea Economic Cooperation Organization
- Collective Security Treaty Organization
- Common Fund for Commodities
- Commonwealth of Independent States
- Community of Portuguese-Speaking Countries
- Community of Sahel-Saharan States
- Conference on Interaction and Confidence-Building Measures in Asia
- Council of Europe
- East African Community
- Economic Community of Central African States
- Economic Community of West African States
- Economic Cooperation Organization
- Energy Charter Conference
- Eurasian Development Bank
- Eurasian Economic Community
- GUUAM (Georgia, Ukraine, Uzbekistan, Azerbaijan and Moldova) Group
- Hague Conference on Private International Law
- Ibero-American Conference
- Indian Ocean Commission
- Inter-American Development Bank
- International Centre for Migration Policy Development
- International Fund for Saving the Aral Sea
- International Hydrographic Organization
- Islamic Development Bank Group
- Italian-Latin American Institute
- Latin American and Caribbean Economic System
- Latin American Integration Association

- Latin American Parliament
- OPEC Fund for International Development
- Organisation of Eastern Caribbean States
- Organization for Economic Co-operation and Development
- Organization for Security and Co-operation in Europe
- Organization of American States
- Pacific Islands Forum
- Permanent Court of Arbitration
- Regional Centre on Small Arms
- Shanghai Cooperation Organization
- South Asian Association for Regional Cooperation
- South Centre
- Southern African Development Community
- World Customs Organization (formerly the Customs Cooperation Council)

Other Entities

The following entities have received standing invitations to participate as observers in the General Assembly and maintain permanent observer offices at the UN headquarters:

- International Committee of the Red Cross
- International Federation of Red Cross and Red Crescent Societies
- Inter-Parliamentary Union
- Sovereign Military Order of Malta
- University for Peace

III. Specialized Agencies and Related Organizations Maintaining Liaison Offices at the UN Headquarters

- Food and Agriculture Organization of the United Nations
- International Atomic Energy Agency
- International Fund for Agricultural Development
- International Labour Organization

- International Monetary Fund
- United Nations Educational, Scientific and Cultural Organization
- United Nations Industrial Development Organization
- World Bank
- World Health Organization
- World Intellectual Property Organization
- World Meteorological Organization
- World Tourism Organization

Appendix B:
Preamble to the Charter of the United Nations

WE THE PEOPLES OF THE UNITED NATIONS DETERMINED

to save succeeding generations from the scourge of war, which twice in our lifetime has brought untold sorrow to mankind, and

to reaffirm faith in fundamental human rights, in the dignity and worth of the human person, in the equal rights of men and women and of nations large and small, and

to establish conditions under which justice and respect for the obligations arising from treaties and other sources of international law can be maintained, and

to promote social progress and better standards of life in larger freedom,

AND FOR THESE ENDS

to practice tolerance and live together in peace with one another as good neighbours, and

to unite our strength to maintain international peace and security, and

to ensure, by the acceptance of principles and the institution of methods, that armed force shall not be used, save in the common interest, and

to employ international machinery for the promotion of the economic and social advancement of all peoples,

HAVE RESOLVED TO COMBINE OUR EFFORTS TO ACCOMPLISH THESE AIMS

Accordingly, our respective Governments, through representatives assembled in the city of San Francisco, who have exhibited their full powers found to be in good and due form, have agreed to the present Charter of the United Nations and do hereby establish an international organization to be known as the United Nations.

GLOSSARY

The following is a list of acronyms and terms that will not only help you in using this book but should serve as reference during your preparations and when at the conference.

AALCO	Asian-African Legal Consultative Organization
ACP	African, Caribbean and Pacific Group of States
ACS	Association of Caribbean States
ADB	Asian Development Bank
AfDB	African Development Bank
ALADI (or LAIA)	Latin American Integration Association (*Asociación Latinoamericana de Integración*)
APEC	Asia-Pacific Economic Cooperation
ASEAN	Association of Southeast Asian Nations
AU	African Union
BSEC	Organization of the Black Sea Economic Cooperation
BTWC (or BWC)	Biological and Toxin Weapons Convention (Biological Weapons Convention) (Convention on the Prohibition of the Development, Production and Stockpiling of Bacteriological (Biological) and Toxin Weapons and on their Destruction)
BWC (or BTWC)	Biological Weapons Convention (Biological and Toxin Weapons Convention) (Convention on the Prohibition of the Development, Production and Stockpiling of Bacteriological (Biological) and Toxin Weapons and on their Destruction)
CACM	Central American Common Market
CAN	Andean Community (*Comunidad Andina*)
CARICOM	Caribbean Community

CCASG (or GCC)	Cooperation Council for the Arab States of the Gulf (Gulf Cooperation Council)
CCPCJ	Commission on Crime Prevention and Criminal Justice
CD	Conference on Disarmament
CDP	Committee for Development Planning
CEMAC	Economic and Monetary Community of Central Africa (*Communauté Économique et Monétaire de l'Afrique Centrale*)
CEN-SAD	Community of Sahel-Saharan States
CFC	Common Fund for Commodities
Chair	Generic name given to the person moderating debate
CICA	Conference on Interaction and Confidence-Building Measures in Asia
CICP	Center for International Crime Prevention
CIS	Commonwealth of Independent States
CND	Commission on Narcotic Drugs
CoE	Council of Europe
COI (or IOC)	Indian Ocean Commission (*Commission de l'Océan Indien*)
Committee	Generic name for each simulation in a conference
COPUOS	Committee on the Peaceful Uses of Outer Space
CPD	Commission on Population and Development
CPLP	Community of Portuguese-Speaking Countries (*Comunidade dos Países de Língua Portuguesa*)
CSD	Commission for Social Development
CSD	Commission on Sustainable Development
CSTO	Collective Security Treaty Organization
CSW	Commission on the Status of Women
CTBTO	Comprehensive Nuclear-Test-Ban Treaty Organization
CTBTO Prep.Com	Preparatory Commission for the Comprehensive Nuclear Test-Ban Treaty Organization

CWC	Chemical Weapons Convention (Convention on the Prohibition of the Development, Production, Stockpiling and Use of Chemical Weapons and on their Destruction)
Dais	The chairing staff of a committee
DDA	Department of Disarmament Affairs
DESA	Department of Economic and Social Affairs
DGACM	Department for General Assembly and Conference Management
DiSec	Disarmament and International Security Committee, First Committee of the General Assembly
DM	Department of Management
DPA	Department of Political Affairs
DPI	Department of Public Information
DPKO	Department of Peacekeeping Operations
DSS	Department of Safety and Security
EAC	East African Community
EAEC (or EurAsEC)	Eurasian Economic Community
EC	European Community
ECA	Economic Commission for Africa
ECCAS	Economic Community of Central African States
ECE	Economic Commission for Europe
ECLAC	Economic Commission for Latin America and the Caribbean
ECO	Economic Cooperation Organization
EcoFin	Economic and Financial Committee, Second Committee of the General Assembly
ECOSOC	Economic and Social Council
ECOWAS	Economic Community of West African States
EDB	Eurasian Development Bank
ESCAP	Economic and Social Commission for Asia and the Pacific
ESCWA	Economic and Social Commission for Western Asia
EU	European Union

EurAsEC (or EAEC)	Eurasian Economic Community
FAO	Food and Agriculture Organization of the United Nations
FSC	Future Security Council
G77	Group of 77
GA	General Assembly
GATT	General Agreement on Tariffs and Trade
GCC (or CCASG)	Gulf Cooperation Council (Cooperation Council for the Arab States of the Gulf)
GRULAC	Group of Latin American and Caribbean States
GUUAM	Georgia, Ukraine, Uzbekistan, Azerbaijan and Moldova (Group)
HCCH	Hague Conference on Private International Law
HRC	United Nations Human Rights Council
HSC	Historical Security Council
IADB (or IDB)	Inter-American Development Bank
IAEA	International Atomic Energy Agency
IBRD	International Bank for Reconstruction and Development
ICAO	International Civil Aviation Organization
ICC	International Criminal Court
ICJ	International Court of Justice
ICMPD	International Centre for Migration Policy Development
ICRC	International Committee of the Red Cross
ICSC	International Civil Service Commission
ICSID	International Centre for Settlement of Investment Disputes
ICTR	International Criminal Tribunal for Rwanda
ICTY	International Criminal Tribunal for the Former Yugoslavia
IDA	International Development Association
IDB (or IADB)	Inter-American Development Bank
IDB	Islamic Development Bank

IDEA	International Institute for Democracy and Electoral Assistance
IDLO	International Development Law Organization
IFAD	International Fund for Agricultural Development
IFAS	International Fund for Saving the Aral Sea
IFC	International Finance Corporation
IFRC	International Federation of Red Cross and Red Crescent Societies
IHO	International Hydrographic Organization
ILAI	Italian-Latin American Institute
ILC	International Law Commission
ILO	International Labour Organization
IMF	International Monetary Fund
IMO	International Maritime Organization
INTERPOL	International Criminal Police Organization
IOC (or COI)	Indian Ocean Commission (*Commission de l'Océan Indien*)
IOM	International Organization for Migration
IPU	Inter-Parliamentary Union
ISA	International Seabed Authority
ISDR	International Strategy for Disaster Reduction
ISO	International Sugar Organization
ITC	International Trade Centre
ITC-ILO	International Training Centre of the ILO
ITLOS	International Tribunal for the Law of the Sea
ITU	International Telecommunication Union
IUCN	International Union for the Conservation of Nature and Natural Resources
LAC	Latin American and Caribbean
LAIA (or ALADI)	Latin American Integration Association (*Asociación Latinoamericana de Integración*)
LAS	League of Arab States (Arab League)
MERCOSUR	Southern Common Market (*Mercado Común del Sur*)
MIGA	Multilateral Investment Guarantee Agency

MINURSO	United Nations Mission for the Referendum in the Western Sahara (*Mission des Nations Unies pour l'Organisation d'un Référendum au Sahara Occidental*)
Model UN	Model United Nations
MONUC	United Nations Organization Mission in the Democratic Republic of the Congo (*Mission de l'Organization des Nations Unies en République démocratique du Congo*)
MUN	Model United Nations
NAFTA	North American Free Trade Agreement
NAM	Non-Aligned Movement
NATO	North Atlantic Treaty Organization
NGO	Non-Governmental Organization
NNPT (or NPT)	Nuclear Non-Proliferation Treaty (Treaty on the Non-Proliferation of Nuclear Weapons)
NPT (or NNPT)	Nuclear Non-Proliferation Treaty (Treaty on the Non-Proliferation of Nuclear Weapons)
OAS	Organization of American States
OAU	Organisation of African Unity (replaced by the African Union)
OCHA	United Nations Office for the Coordination of Humanitarian Affairs
OECD	Organisation for Economic Co-operation and Development
OECS	Organisation of Eastern Caribbean States
OFID	OPEC Fund for International Development
OHCHR	Office of the High Commissioner for Human Rights
OHRLLS	Office of the High Representative for the Least Developed Countries, Landlocked Developing Countries and Small Island Developing States
OIC	Organisation of the Islamic Conference
OIOS	Office of Internal Oversight Services
OLA	Office of Legal Affairs

OPANAL	Agency for the Prohibition of Nuclear Weapons in Latin America and the Caribbean (*Organismo para la Proscripción de las Armas Nucleares en la América Latina y el Caribe*)
OPCW	Organisation for the Prohibition of Chemical Weapons
OPEC	Organization of the Petroleum Exporting Countries
OSCE	Organization for Security and Co-operation in Europe
OSG	Office of the Secretary-General
Parlatino	Latin American Parliament (*Parlamento Latinoamericano*)
PC	Press Corps
PCA	Permanent Court of Arbitration
PIF	Pacific Islands Forum
PPD	Partners in Population and Development
Proposal	Term used to refer to any substantive or procedural motion
RECSA	Regional Centre on Small Arms
SAARC	South Asian Association for Regional Cooperation
SADC	Southern African Development Community
SC	Security Council
SCO	Shanghai Cooperation Organisation
SELA	Latin American and Caribbean Economic System (*Sistema Económico Latinoamericano y del Caribe*)
SG	Secretary-General
SICA	Central American Integration System (*Sistema de la Integración Centroamericana*)
Simple majority	50% plus one vote
SMOM	Sovereign Military Order of Malta
SocHum	Social, Humanitarian and Cultural Affairs Committee, Third Committee of the General Assembly
Soviet Union	Union of Soviet Socialist Republics (USSR)
SpecPol	Special Political and Decolonization Committee, Fourth Committee of the General Assembly

Substantive motions	Resolutions and amendments
TC	Trusteeship Council
UN	United Nations
UN-HABITAT	United Nations Human Settlements Programme
UN-INSTRAW	United Nations International Research and Training Institute for the Advancement of Women
UNA-USA	United Nations Association of the United States of America
UNAIDS	Joint United Nations Programme on HIV/AIDS
UNAMSIL	United Nations Mission in Sierra Leone
UNCCD	United Nations Convention to Combat Desertification
UNCDF	United Nations Capital Development Fund
UNCED	United Nations Conference on Environment and Development
UNCITRAL	United Nations Commission of International Trade Law
UNCTAD	United Nations Conference on Trade and Development
UNDCP	United Nations International Drug Control Programme
UNDEF	United Nations Democracy Fund
UNDHA	United Nations Department of Humanitarian Affairs
UNDOF	United Nations Disengagement Observer Force
UNDP	United Nations Development Programme
UNEP	United Nations Environment Programme
UNESCO	United Nations Educational, Scientific and Cultural Organization
UNFICYP	United Nations Peacekeeping Force in Cyprus
UNFIP	United Nations Fund for International Partnerships
UNFPA	United Nations Population Fund (formerly the United Nations Fund for Population Assistance)
UNHCHR	United Nations High Commissioner for Human Rights
UNHCR	United Nations High Commissioner for Refugees

UNIC	United Nations Information Centre
UNICEF	United Nations Children's Fund
UNICRI	United Nations Interregional Crime and Justice Research Institute
UNIDIR	United Nations Institute for Disarmament Research
UNIDO	United Nations Industrial Development Organization
UNIFEM	United Nations Development Fund for Women
UNIFIL	United Nations Interim Force in Lebanon
UNIKOM	United Nations Iraq-Kuwait Observation Mission
UNITAR	United Nations Institute for Training and Research
UNMEE	United Nations Mission in Ethiopia and Eritrea
UNMIBH	United Nations Mission in Bosnia and Herzegovina
UNMIK	United Nations Mission in Kosovo
UNMISET	United Nations Mission of Support in East Timor
UNMOGIP	United Nations Military Observer Group in India and Pakistan
UNMOP	United Nations Mission of Observers in Prevlaka
UNODC	United Nations Office on Drugs and Crime
UNOG	United Nations Office at Geneva
UNOMIG	United Nations Observer Mission in Georgia
UNON	United Nations Office at Nairobi
UNOOSA	United Nations Office for Outer Space Affairs
UNOPS	United Nations Office for Project Services
UNOV	United Nations Office at Vienna
UNPA	United Nations Postal Administration
UNRISD	United Nations Research Institute for Social Development
UNRWA	United Nations Relief and Works Agency for Palestine Refugees in the Near East
UNSD	United Nations Statistics Division
UNSSC	United Nations System Staff College
UNTAET	United Nations Transitional Administration in East Timor
UNTSO	United Nations Truce Supervision Organization

UNU	United Nations University
UNV	United Nations Volunteers
UNWTO	World Tourism Organization
UPU	Universal Postal Union
USSR	Union of Soviet Socialist Republics (Soviet Union)
WB	World Bank
WCO	World Customs Organization
WEOG	Western European and Other States Group
WEU	Western European Union
WFP	United Nations World Food Programme
WHO	World Health Organization
WIPO	World Intellectual Property Organization
WMO	World Meteorological Organization
WTO	World Trade Organization

INDEX

CPSIA information can be obtained at www.ICGtesting.com
Printed in the USA
BVOW03s0357230714

360166BV00007B/205/P